1985 Supplement

CRIMINAL LAW AND ITS PROCESSES

1985 Supplement

Kadish, Schulhofer, and Paulsen
CRIMINAL LAW AND ITS PROCESSES
Cases and Materials

Fourth Edition

Sanford H. Kadish
Alexander F. and May R. Morrison Professor of Law
University of California, Berkeley

Stephen J. Schulhofer
Ferdinand Wakeman Hubbell Professor of Law
University of Pennsylvania

Little, Brown and Company *Boston and Toronto*

Library of Congress Catalog Card No. 82-081495

ISBN 0-316-47814-8

Third Printing

FG

Published simultaneously in Canada
by Little, Brown & Company (Canada) Limited

PRINTED IN THE UNITED STATES OF AMERICA

Contents

Table of Cases

Italics indicate principal cases. Asterisked page references indicate location where a case is quoted from or discussed at some length.

Table of Cases

Chapter One

The Structure of the Criminal Justice System

Page 6. At the end of footnote c add:

The population subject to correctional supervision has grown at a striking rate over the past few years. As of the end of 1983, there were 419,820 prisoners in state or federal custody, an increase of about 39 percent since 1979. In addition, as of June 1983 a record 223,551 persons were held in local jails, a 41 percent increase over the total of the last jail census in February 1978. At the end of 1983 the adult probation population stood at 1,502,247 (an increase of 38 percent over the 1979 figure), and the parole population stood at 251,708 (an increase of 15 percent over the 1979 figure). See U.S. Department of Justice, Bureau of Justice Statistics, Bulletin: The 1983 Jail Census (Nov. 1984); U.S. Department of Justice, Bureau of Justice Statistics, Bulletin: Probation and Parole 1983 (Sept. 1984). Apparently parole populations have grown more slowly than either prison or probation populations, as a consequence of increased emphasis on the use of determinate sentencing and decreased reliance on discretionary prison release decisions by parole boards. See Casebook pages 1117-1126.

Page 10. At the end of footnote g insert:

The Bail Reform Act of 1984, 18 U.S.C. §§1341-1350, expressly authorizes preventive detention prior to trial in federal criminal prosecutions, on a finding that "no condition or conditions [of release] will reasonably assure the appearance of the [defendant] as required and the safety of any other person and the community." §3142(e). Unlike the earlier D.C. legislation, Casebook page 10n.g, the federal statute does not permit judges to insure detention by setting high money bail on the pretext of "risk of flight"; §3142(c) specifies that the "judicial officer may not impose a financial condition that results in the pretrial detention of the person." The statute thus appears to contemplate that detention prior to trial will occur only after compliance with the specific procedural requirements of the preventive detention hearing, and as a result such hearings have been held with some frequency. To date, several Courts of Appeals have upheld the constitutionality of the preventive detention provisions. See, e.g., United States v. Delker, 37 Crim. L. Rptr. 2001 (3d Cir., March 18, 1985); United States v. Jessup, 36 Crim. L. Rptr. 2445 (1st Cir., Feb. 25, 1985).

Chapter Two

How Guilt Is Established

Page 28. After line 14 add:

AKE v. OKLAHOMA

Supreme Court of the United States
105 S. Ct. 1087 (1985)

MARSHALL, J., delivered the opinion of the Court. . . .

Late in 1979, Glen Burton Ake was arrested and charged with murdering a couple and wounding their two children. . . . His behavior at arraignment, and in other prearraignment incidents at the jail, was so bizarre that the trial judge *sua sponte* ordered him to be examined by a psychiatrist. . . . The examining psychiatrist . . . diagnosed Ake as a probable paranoid schizophrenic and recommended a prolonged psychiatric evaluation to determine whether Ake was competent to stand trial.

In March, Ake was committed to a state hospital to be examined with respect to his "present sanity," i.e., his competency to stand trial. On April 10, less than six months after the incidents for which Ake was indicted, the chief forensic psychiatrist at the state hospital informed the court that Ake was not competent to stand trial. . . . The court found Ake to be a "mentally ill person in need of care and treatment" and incompetent to stand trial, and ordered him committed to the state mental hospital.

Six weeks later, the chief forensic psychiatrist informed the court that Ake had become competent to stand trial. At the time, Ake was receiving 200 milligrams of Thorazine, an antipsychotic drug, three times daily, and the psychiatrist indicated that, if Ake continued to receive that dosage, his condition would remain stable. The State then resumed proceedings against Ake.

At a pretrial conference in June, Ake's attorney informed the court that his client would raise an insanity defense. To enable him to prepare and present such a defense adequately, the attorney stated, a psychiatrist would have to examine Ake with respect to his mental condition at the time of the offense. During Ake's 3-month stay at the state hospital, no inquiry had been made into his sanity at the time of the offense, and, as an indigent, Ake could not afford to pay for a psychiatrist. . . . The trial judge . . . denied the motion for a psychiatric evaluation at state expense. . . .

Ake was tried for two counts of murder in the first degree, a crime punishable by death in Oklahoma, and for two counts of shooting with intent to kill. At the guilt phase of trial, his sole defense was insanity. Although defense counsel called to the stand and questioned each of the psychiatrists who had examined Ake at the state hospital, none testified about his mental state at the time of the offense because none had examined him on that point. The prosecution, in turn, asked each of these psychiatrists whether he had performed or seen the results of any examination diagnosing Ake's mental state at the time of the offense, and each doctor replied that he had not. *As a result, there was no expert testimony for either side on Ake's sanity at the time of the offense.* The jurors were then instructed that . . . Ake was to be presumed sane at the time of the crime unless *he* presented evidence sufficient to raise a reasonable doubt about his sanity at that time. If he raised such a doubt in their minds, the jurors were informed, the burden of proof shifted to the State to prove sanity beyond a reasonable doubt. The jury rejected Ake's insanity defense and returned a verdict of guilty on all counts.

. . . The jury sentenced Ake to death on each of the two murder counts, and to 500 years' imprisonment on each of the two counts of shooting with intent to kill.

. . . [T]he Oklahoma Court of Criminal Appelas . . . affirmed the convictions and sentences. We granted certiorari. . . .

This Court has long recognized that when a State brings its judicial power to bear on an indigent defendant in a criminal proceeding, it must take steps to assure that the defendant has a fair opportunity to present his defense. . . . [J]ustice cannot be equal where, simply as a result of his poverty, a defendant is denied the opportunity to participate meaningfully in a judicial proceeding in which his liberty is at stake. . . .

Meaningful access to justice has been the consistent theme of these cases. . . . [A] criminal trial is fundamentally unfair if the State proceeds against an indigent defendant without making certain that he has access to the raw materials integral to the building of an effective defense. . . .

. . . In this case we must decide whether, and under what conditions, the participation of a psychiatrist is important enough to preparation of a defense to require the State to provide an indigent defendant with access to competent psychiatric assistance in preparing the defense. Three factors are relevant to this determination. The first is the private interest that will be affected by the action of the State. The second is the governmental interest that will be affected if the safeguard is to be provided. The third is the probable value of the additional or substitute procedural safeguards that are sought, and the risk of an erroneous deprivation of the affected interest if those safeguards are not provided. See Mathews v. Eldridge, 424 U.S. 319, 335 (1976). . . .

The private interest in the accuracy of a criminal proceeding that places an individual's life or liberty at risk is almost uniquely compelling. . . .

We consider, next, the interest of the State. Oklahoma asserts that to provide Ake with psychiatric assistance on the record before us would result in a staggering burden to the State. We are unpersuaded by this assertion. Many States, as well as the Federal Government, currently make psychiatric assistance available to indigent defendants, and they have not found the financial burden so great as to preclude this assistance. This is especially so when the obligation of the State is limited to provision of one competent psychiatrist, as it is in many States, and as we limit the right we recognize today.[a] . . .

Last, we inquire into the probable value of the psychiatric assistance sought, and the risk of error in the proceeding if such assistance is not offered. . . .

. . . [W]hen the State has made the defendant's mental condition relevant to his criminal culpability and to the punishment he might suffer, the assistance of a psychiatrist may well be crucial to the defendant's ability to marshal his defense. . . . [W]ithout the assistance of a psychiatrist to conduct a professional examination on issues relevant to the defense, to help determine whether the insanity defense is viable, to present testimony, and to assist in preparing the cross-examination of a State's psychiatric witnesses, the risk of an inaccurate resolution of sanity issues is extremely high. . . .

A defendant's mental condition is not necessarily at issue in every criminal proceeding, however, and it is unlikely that psychiatric assistance of the kind we have described would be of probable value in cases where it is not. . . .

We therefore hold that when a defendant demonstrates to the trial judge that his sanity at the time of the offense is to be a significant

---

a. Query: Why? Is it clear that in a case such as *Chavis* [Casebook page 28], the defendant should never have a right to examination by a second psychiatrist? — EDS.

factor at trial, the State must, at a minimum, assure the defendant access to a competent psychiatrist who will conduct an appropriate examination and assist in evaluation, preparation, and presentation of the defense. This is not to say, of course, that the indigent defendant has a constitutional right to choose a psychiatrist of his personal liking or to receive funds to hire his own. Our concern is that the indigent defendant have access to a competent psychiatrist for the purpose we have discussed, and as in the case of the provision of counsel we leave to the States the decision on how to implement this right.

On the record before us, it is clear that Ake's mental state at the time of the offense was a substantial factor in his defense, and that the trial court was on notice of that fact when the request for a court-appointed psychiatrist was made. . . .

Accordingly, we reverse and remand for a new trial.

It is so ordered.

BURGER, C.J., concurring in the judgment.

. . . In capital cases the finality of the sentence imposed warrants protections that may or may not be required in other cases. Nothing in the Court's opinion reaches non-capital cases.[b]

REHNQUIST, J., dissenting.

. . . [T]he constitutional rule announced by the Court is far too broad. I would limit the rule to capital cases, and make clear that the entitlement is to an independent psychiatric evaluation, not to a defense consultant.

. . . Under Oklahoma law, the burden is initially on the defendant to raise a reasonable doubt as to his sanity at the time of the offense. Once that burden is satisfied, the burden shifts to the State to prove sanity beyond a reasonable doubt. Since the State introduced *no* evidence concerning Ake's sanity at the time of the offense, it seems clear that as a matter of state law Ake failed to carry the initial burden. . . .

Nor is this a surprising conclusion on the facts here. The evidence of the brutal murders perpetrated on the victims, and of the month-long crime spree following the murders, would not seem to raise any question of sanity unless one were to adopt the dubious doctrine that no one in his right mind would commit a murder. . . . The Court apparently would infer from the fact that Ake was diagnosed as mentally ill some six months after the offense that there was a reasonable doubt as

---

b. Would the majority accept this reading of its opinion? — EDS.

to his ability to know right from wrong when he committed it. But even the experts were unwilling to draw this inference.[c]

Before holding that the State is obligated to furnish the services of a psychiatric witness to an indigent defendant who reasonably contests his sanity at the time of the offense, I would require a considerably greater showing than this. And even then I do not think due process is violated merely because an indigent lacks sufficient funds to pursue a state-law defense as thoroughly as he would like. . . . It is highly doubtful that due process requires a State to make available an insanity defense to a criminal defendant, but in any event if such a defense is afforded the burden of proving insanity can be placed on the defendant. See Patterson v. New York, 432 U.S. 197 (1977). That is essentially what happened here, and Ake failed to carry his burden under state law. . . .

Finally, even if I were to agree with the Court that some right to a state-appointed psychiatrist should be recognized here, I would not grant the broad right to "access to a competent psychiatrist who will conduct an appropriate examination *and assist in evaluation, preparation, and presentation of the defense.*" Ante. A psychiatrist is not an attorney, whose job it is to advocate. His opinion is sought on a question that the State of Oklahoma treats as a question of *fact.* Since any "unfairness" in these cases would arise from the fact that the only competent witnesses on the question are being hired by the State, all the defendant should be entitled to is one competent opinion—whatever the witness' conclusion—from a psychiatrist who acts independently of the prosecutor's office. Although the independent psychiatrist should be available to answer defense counsel's questions prior to trial, and to testify if called, I see no reason why the defendant should be entitled to an opposing view, or to a "defense" advocate.

For the foregoing reasons, I would affirm the judgment of the Court of Criminal Appeals of Oklahoma.

PROBLEM

Should the right to an appointed psychiatrist, recognized in *Ake,* be extended to requests for other experts? In Caldwell v. Mississippi, 443

---

c. Note that in Jones v. United States, Supplement page 90 infra, a five-justice majority that included Justice Rehnquist held that if insanity existed at the time of an offense, the insanity may be presumed to continue through the time of trial and indefinitely thereafter. Is there a good reason why insanity at the time of an offense should be presumed to continue through the time of trial, but insanity at the time of trial should not be presumed to have existed at the time of the offense? Is Justice Rehnquist's position in *Ake* consistent with his position in *Jones?* — EDS.

So. 2d 806 (1983), the court denied a defendant's request for appoint-
ment of a ballistics expert to assist in preparation of his defense in a
capital murder trial. Although the crucial issue at trial was the identification of the assailant, and although a ballistics expert testified for the
prosecution, the court said that the only assistance to indigent defendants that is constitutionally required "is the assistance of legal counsel," and added that the defendant had failed to specify the cost or the
specific value of the expert he sought to hire. Id. at 812. The Supreme
Court has granted certiorari. 105 S. Ct. 243 (1984). How should *Caldwell* be decided?

Page 41. At the end of line 3 add:

Rules 403 and 404(b) of the Federal Rules of Evidence illustrate one
rigorous statement of these principles:

> RULE 403. . . .
> Although relevant, evidence may be excluded if its probative value is
> substantially outweighed by the danger of unfair prejudice, confusion of the
> issues, or misleading the jury, or by considerations of undue delay, waste of
> time, or needless presentation of cumulative evidence.
> RULE 404. . . .
> (b) Other crimes, wrongs, or acts. Evidence of other crimes, wrongs, or
> acts is not admissible to prove the character of a person in order to show
> that he acted in conformity therewith. It may, however, be admissible for
> other purposes, such as proof of motive, opportunity, intent, preparation,
> plan, knowledge, identity, or absence of mistake or accident.

Page 44. Before "Note on the Effectiveness of Jury Instructions" insert:

For a helpful discussion see Uviller, Evidence of Character to Prove
Conduct: Illusion, Illogic and Injustice in the Courtroom, 130 U. Pa. L.
Rev. 845 (1982).

Page 45. In footnote 30, at the end of the first paragraph, insert:

Spencer was explicitly reaffirmed in Marshall v. Lonberger, 103 S. Ct.
843, 853 n.6 (1983). Four justices, in a dissent written by Justice Stevens, argued that the premises underlying *Spencer* can no longer be
considered valid and that that decision should be reexamined.

Page 57. At the end of footnote 43 insert:

In People v. Hayes, 36 Crim. L. Rptr. 2416 (March 6, 1985), a divided
Michigan Supreme Court held that a defendant may be precluded from

raising an insanity defense if he does not cooperate during a court-ordered psychiatric examination. The dissenters argued that this result forces a defendant to relinquish one constitutional right (his privilege against compulsory self-incrimination) in order to assert another (his right to present evidence negating an element of the offense charged). Query: What result if defense counsel argues that the defendant's failure to cooperate is itself a product of his mental disorder?

Page 107. Before "2. *Constitutional implications*" insert:

The federal rule, which precludes an attack on inconsistent jury verdicts, was reaffirmed in United States v. Powell, 105 S. Ct. 471 (1984). Justice Rehnquist, speaking for a unanimous Court, noted (id. at 477):

> Inconsistent verdicts . . . present a situation where "error," in the sense that the jury has not followed the court's instructions, most certainly has occurred, but it is unclear whose ox has been gored. Given this uncertainty, and the fact that the Government is precluded from challenging the acquittal, it is hardly satisfactory to allow the defendant to receive a new trial on the conviction as a matter of course. . . . For us, the possibility that the inconsistent verdicts may favor the criminal defendant as well as the Government militates against review of such convictions at the defendant's behest. . . .

Page 121. After line 7 insert:

1a. Subsequent developments. For a helpful discussion of the foregoing issues, see Note, Identifying and Remedying Ineffective Assistance of Criminal Defense Counsel: A New Look after *United States v. Decoster,* 93 Harv. L. Rev. 752 (1980). A useful discussion of the special problems of effective assistance in capital cases appears in Goodpaster, The Trial for Life: Effective Assistance of Counsel in Death Penalty Cases, 58 N.Y.U.L. Rev. 299 (1983).

STRICKLAND v. WASHINGTON, 104 S. Ct. 2052 (1984): [Defendant, charged with a series of brutal murders and numerous related crimes, was convicted on three counts of capital murder and sentenced to death. In habeas corpus proceedings, the United States Court of Appeals for the Eleventh Circuit (1) noted serious doubts about whether defendant's trial lawyer had conducted an adequate investigation; (2) articulated standards to guide the determination of whether and when counsel may properly decline to investigate a plausible line of defense; and (3) held that in the event of a failure to satisfy those standards, the defendant would also have to prove "actual and substantial disadvantage to the course of his defense" in order to win the right to a new trial. The court ordered an evidentiary hearing to determine whether there had been ineffective assistance in accordance with these criteria. The Supreme Court reversed and held that the writ of habeas corpus should be denied. Writing for seven members of the Court, Justice O'CONNOR said:]

. . . No particular set of detailed rules for counsel's conduct can satisfactorily take account of the variety of circumstances faced by defense counsel or the range of legitimate decisions regarding how best to represent a criminal defendant. Any such set of rules would interfere with the constitutionally protected independence of counsel and restrict the wide latitude counsel must have in making tactical decisions. See United States v. Decoster, 624 F.2d, at 208. . . .

Judicial scrutiny of counsel's performance must be highly deferential. . . . Because of the difficulties inherent in making the evaluation, a court must indulge a strong presumption that counsel's conduct falls within the wide range of reasonable professional assistance; that is, the defendant must overcome the presumption that, under the circumstances, the challenged action "might be considered sound trial strategy."

These standards require no special amplification in order to define counsel's duty to investigate, the duty at issue in this case. . . . In any ineffectiveness case, a particular decision not to investigate must be directly assessed for reasonableness in all the circumstances, applying a heavy measure of deference to counsel's judgments.

. . . [Moreover,] any deficiencies in counsel's performance must be prejudicial to the defense in order to constitute ineffective assistance under the Constitution.

It is not enough for the defendant to show that the errors had some conceivable effect on the outcome of the proceeding. . . .

On the other hand, we believe that a defendant need not show that counsel's deficient conduct more likely than not altered the outcome in the case. . . . The defendant must show that there is a reasonable probability that, but for counsel's unprofessional errors, the result of the proceeding would have been different. A reasonable probability is a probability sufficient to undermine confidence in the outcome.

[Justice BRENNAN concurred in Court's discussion of the standards for determining ineffective assistance but dissented from the result. Justice MARSHALL dissented.]

Page 129. After line 4 add:

Rule 3.3 was approved by the ABA House of Delegates at its July/August 1983 meeting. The "caveat" no longer appears in the body of Rule 3.3 but is included in the commentary. See 52 U.S.L.W. 17-18 (Aug. 16, 1983).

Page 132. After the second full paragraph insert:

At least one recent decision casts some doubt on the permissibility of the passive approach. In State v. Lee, 36 Crim. L. Rptr. 2038 (Ariz., Sept. 25, 1984), defense counsel acquiesced in his client's desire to call a witness who the attorney believed would give perjured testimony; the attorney then declined to make a closing argument. The Arizona Supreme Court held that this course of conduct amounted to ineffective assistance of counsel. Can the attorney avoid the difficulty by refusing to call the witness in the first place? Or should the attorney attempt to make a closing argument that does not rely on the witness's testimony?

PROBLEM

Prior to his murder trial, defendant advised his attorney that at the moment he stabbed the deceased, he thought that the deceased had been reaching for a gun that the deceased reputedly owned. The defendant stated, however, that he had not actually seen the gun. Later, after efforts to find a gun in deceased's apartment had failed, defendant told his attorney that he had seen something "metallic" in the deceased's hands just before the stabbing. Convinced that the defendant had concocted this story to bolster his self-defense claim, the attorney told his client that if he insisted on testifying that he had seen a gun, he (the attorney) would move to withdraw, would advise the state trial judge that the testimony was perjurious, and would testify against the defendant. Defendant then chose to testify only that he thought that the deceased had a gun. His self-defense claim was rejected, and he was convicted a second-degree murder. Questions: Did the defense attorney handle the problem properly? Was the defendant deprived of the effective assistance of counsel? See Whiteside v. Scurr, 744 F.2d 1323 (8th Cir. 1984), cert. granted, 53 U.S.L.W. 3739 (April 15, 1985).

Page 155. Before "2. Guilty pleas and sentencing concessions" insert:

In Philadelphia the felony guilty plea rate is only about 45 percent. Most felony cases are tried before a judge without a jury, and these trials are not "slow pleas" but rather are fully contested adversary proceedings. See Schulhofer, Is Plea Bargaining Inevitable?, 97 Harv. L. Rev. (1984). On the basis of these findings, the author argues that plea bargaining is not necessary for the effective management of heavy criminal caseloads, even in large urban jurisdictions.

Page 197. After the first full paragraph add:

For a critique of utilitarian approaches to deterrence and a thoughtful exploration of the relationship between retributive conceptions and the deterrence problem, see Seidman, Soldiers, Martyrs, and Criminals: Utilitarian Theory and the Problem of Crime Control, 94 Yale L.J. 315 (1984).

Chapter Three
The Justification of Punishment

Page 210. After line 8 insert the following new section:

5. Incapacitation

COHEN, INCAPACITATING CRIMINALS: RECENT RESEARCH FINDINGS

U.S. Department of Justice, National Institute of Justice, Research in Brief *(December 1983)*

Increased attention given in recent years to incapacitation as a crime control strategy, and as a purpose of sentencing, stems from a number of factors:

- confidence has waned in the ability of correctional programs to rehabilitate offenders
- public attitudes toward crime and criminals have become more punitive
- prisons throughout the United States are crowded, having reached an all-time peak population of 431,829 on June 30, 1983
- recent research efforts suggest that it may be possible to identify and incarcerate high-rate offenders, thereby promising an eventual ability to reduce crime without crowding the prisons.

Researchers and public policy advocates distinguish between *collective incapacitation* and *selective incapacitation*. Under *collective* strategies, all persons convicted of a designated offense, say robbery or any second felony conviction, would receive the same sentence, say 5 years. Research has shown that the reduction in crime that would result from such policies is limited and that prison populations would increase dramatically if such policies were systematically pursued.

Selective strategies would involve individualized sentences based on predictions that particular offenders would commit serious offenses at a high rate if not incaracerated. A recent RAND Corporation report[a] concludes that use of such predictions could reduce crime with little or no increase in prison populations. However, other major researchers assert that the Greenwood work has serious limitations and that the best available prediction methods are simply not good enough to serve as the basis of a system of selective incapacitation. . . .

Collective Incapacitation

. . . Offenders who are imprisoned are unable to commit crimes in the free community. Thus, all imprisonment is incapacitative and should result in the commission of fewer crimes. . . .

. . . By checking the past criminal records of persons currently convicted of crimes, it is possible to determine which current offenders would have been imprisoned under, say, a mandatory 5-year sentencing policy for all violent felonies, and to conclude that the current offense would not have been committed.

Table 2 summarizes the findings of the major published research on

TABLE 2
Estimates of the Collective Incapacitative Effect of Alternative Imprisonment Policies

Study	Data base	Alternative sentencing policy: five-year mandatory prison terms	Target offense	Estimated incapacitated effect: reduction in target offense
Van Dine et al. (1977, 1979)	Arrestees in Franklin County, Ohio, during 1973	After any felony conviction as an adult	Murder, rape, robbery, and aggravated assault	17.4%
		After repeat felony convictions as an adult	Same	6
Petersilia and Greenwood (1978)	Convictions in Denver District Court, between 1968 and 1970	After any felony convictions as an adult	Murder, kidnapping, rape, robbery, and aggravated assault	31
		"	Burglary	42
		After repeat felong convictions as an adult	Violent offenses	16
		"	Burglary	15
Cohen (1982)	Arrestees in Washington, D.C. during 1973	After any conviction for a "criterion" offense as in adult	"Criterion" offenses (index offenses other than larceny)	13.7
		After repeat conviction for a "criterion" offense as an adult	Same	3.8

a. P. Greenwood, with A. Abrahamse, Selective Incapacitation: Report to the National Institute of Justice (1982). — EDS.

the likely crime reduction effects of various hypothetical sentencing policies.

The most striking finding is that incapacitation does not appear to achieve large reductions in crime. . . . [T]he estimated crime reduction effect is in the 10-20 percent range. This is not insubstantial, representing from 131,000 to 262,000 reported violent index offenses in the United States during 1980. Nonetheless, incapacitation does not make the dent in crime that might have been expected from a "lock-em-up" strategy.

In part, this is because incapacitation policies can prevent only the subsequent crimes of convicted offenders who are eligible for incarceration. Many people charged with crimes, however, have not been convicted before. In Cohen's District of Columbia study,[b] for example, 76 percent of adult arrestees had not previously been convicted of the offenses studied. Thus, at most, only 24 percent of the current adult arrests could have been prevented by imposing lengthy prison terms at the time of the earlier conviction.

. . . Although the effects of collective incapacitation on crime reduction are low, the effects on prison populations are likely to be substantial. Table 3 shows the probable impact on prison populations of 5-year mandatory prison sentences for selected offenses for several of the jurisdictions shown in Table 2. Prison populations would be doubled, tripled, or even more dramatically increased.

TABLE 3

Impact on Prison Populations of Mandatory Five-Year Prison Terms after Conviction

Study	Jurisdiction	Target offenses	Expected increase in prison population for target offenses (%)
Petersilia and Greenwood (1978)	Denver, Colorado, 1968-70	Any felony convictions	450
Van Dine et al. (1979)	Franklin County, Ohio, 1973	Any felony convictions	523
Cohen (1982)	Washington, D.C., 1973	Convictions for any index offense other than larceny	310

b. Cohen, Patterns of Adult Offending (unpublished Ph.D. dissertation, 1982). — EDS.

Thus, the research demonstrates that broadly based collective incapacitation policies involving lengthy prison sentences for serious crimes are not feasible. . . .

Selective Incapacitation

It is frequently observed that a small number of offenders commits a disproportionately large number of offenses. If prison resources can be effectively targeted to high-rate offenders, it should be possible to achieve current, or improved, levels of crime control with reduced numbers in prison. The key to such a policy rests on an ability to identify high-rate offenders prospectively, and at relatively early stages in their careers.

Recent selective incapacitation research has stimulated considerable controversy. Some of the debate has focused on ethical implications of selective incapacitation and some has focused on limitations of the existing research.

ETHICAL CONCERNS

A key element of selective incapacitation is that some offenders would be imprisoned for a longer period than others convicted of the same offense, because of predictions about their *future* criminality. Reactions to selective incapacitation proposals are influenced by differing views about the purposes of criminal punishments. Proponents argue that persons convicted of crimes can justly receive any lawful sentence (unless, perhaps, it is so disproportionately severe as to be unjust), and that holding some offenders longer than others for predictive reasons raises no significant ethical problems. Moreover, proponents point out that existing sentencing is implicitly incapacitative: presumably, most judges and other officials base their decisions in part on their beliefs about an offender's future dangerousness. From this perspective, selective incapacitation policies are preferable to existing practice because predictions of future crime would no longer be ad hoc and idiosyncratic, but would be based upon the best available scientific evidence.

Some critics argue against selective incapacitation in principle: punishment should be *deserved* and two persons who have committed the same offense deserve equal punishment. If selective incapacitation means that one person will be held longer than another because of predictions of future crimes, it is unjust.

Other critics—including people who in principle do not object to unequal punishments—offer other objections:

1. It is *unfair* to punish people for crimes they have not yet committed, and might not commit if released.

2. It is unjust to incarcerate (or further incarcerate) people on the basis of predictions of future crime because those predictions are too often *wrong*—typically two out of three persons so identified are "false positives," people who would not have committed future crimes even if released.
3. Many of the variables in prediction formulas (see Table 4 showing the RAND variables) raise other policy or ethical questions. For example, several of the RAND variables involve juvenile records, which many believe should not be admissible in relation to adult prosecutions. For another example, the RAND formula includes employment information, which many would exclude from consideration at sentencing, along with education and similar factors, as class-based variables that, in effect, discriminate against the poor.
4. Many prediction variables, like education, employment, and residential stability, are associated with race: some minorities are on average less well educated and less stably employed than the white majority. Building such variables into sentencing standards, while not intended to punish minorities more severely, would have that effect. . .

EMPIRICAL PROBLEMS IN PREDICTION

Efforts at predicting future crimes have not been very successful. In recent review of efforts to predict violance, John Monahan (1981) reports that the best predictions have false-positive rates of over 60 percent; of every three individuals predicted to be violent in the future, two were *not* observed to be violent.

Greenwood's selective incapacitation research focused on inmates currently convicted for robbery or burglary. The inmates were divided into low-, medium-, and high-rate offenders for robbery and burglary on the basis of armed robberies and burglaries they admitted committing during the time they were free in the 2 years preceding the current incarceration. Using one variable at a time, a variety of other characteristics were then examined for their association with individual crime rates. Seven variables (see Table 4) were selected to form a

TABLE 4

Variables Used in Scale to Distinguish Inmates by Individual Crime Rates

1. Prior conviction for same charge
2. Incarcerated more than 50 percent of preceding two years
3. Convicted before age sixteen
4. Served time in state juvenile facility
5. Drug use in preceding two years
6. Drug use as juvenile
7. Employed less than 50 percent of preceding two years

simple additive scale for distinguishing offenders. Using this scale as a basis for imposing long prison terms for predicted high-rate offenders, Greenwood estimated that the number of robberies by adults in California could be reduced by 20 percent with only 2.5 percent increase in total prison population.

These results are an important illustration of the *potential* of selective incapacitation policies. The research, however, has a number of serious methodological and practical shortcomings:

1. The analysis was entirely *retrospective*, starting with known high-rate offenders and looking only at their past admitted crimes. There is no way to judge the scale's accuracy in prospectively identifying high-rate offenders.
2. The scale lacks *internal validation*. It is unknown how it would work if applied to another group of apparently comparable high-rate imprisoned offenders.
3. The scale lacks *external validation*. Since the research involved only *incaracerated* offenders, it is unknown how useful it would be for judges having to decide *whether* to incarcerate.
4. The scale relies heavily on self-reported information. At sentencing, one could not confidently rely on information provided by the offender.
5. The Greenwood scale correctly identified 45 percent of the high-rate offenders, the true positives. In other words, the false positive rate was 55 percent, close to that found by Monahan to characterize violence predictions generally.

. . . Given the crucial issues of low predictive accuracy and the tentativeness of the estimated impacts characterizing this research, there is as yet no sound basis for implementing selective incapacitation policies.

Criminal Career Incapacitation

A different approach to incapacitation, based on criminal career patterns, may avoid some of the problems associated with selective incapacitation. This approach relies on recent empirical research on criminal careers. . . .

The goal is to identify classes of offenders who, on average, would remain active at high rates. In Blumstein and Cohen's analysis of criminal career patterns for arrestees in Washington, D.C.,[c] convicted robbery and burglary defendants emerged as prime candidates for inca-

---

c. Blumstein & Cohen, Estimation of Individual Crime Rates from Arrest Records, 70 J. Crim. L. & C. 561 (1979). —EDS.

pacitation. They commit these offenses, on average, at relatively high rates, and have relatively short careers. Short prison terms for these offenders have the potential to avert large portions of their expected careers and thereby to reduce robbery and burglary rates. . . .

Minimum 2-year terms imposed on all adult defendants convicted of robbery would result in an 8 percent reduction in robberies by adults, while increasing the total prison population by 7 percent.

Like Greenwood's selective incapacitation research, this alternative approach is at an early stage. However, if it can be perfected, it may avoid some of the ethical pitfalls of selective incapacitation. Being based solely on present and past criminal records, it is less susceptible to attack for reliance on controversial personal variables, and since sentencing policies would apply uniformly to groups of similar offenders — a form of targeted collective incapacitation — objections of unjust, unequal punishment have less force. . . .

NOTES

1. Would a "collective incapacitation" strategy be acceptable if it could in fact achieve a very substantial reduction in crime rates? (Consider, for example, the estimated 42 percent reduction in burglary rates claimed in one of the studies reported in Table 2 of the Cohen article.) Is society unwilling to pay the cost (in terms of increased prison populations) of achieving such a reduction in crime? Or is such a strategy unacceptable for ethical reasons unrelated to cost?

2. Is Cohen's proposal for a strategy of "criminal career incapacitation" also subject to ethical objections relating either to the proportion of false positives or to the requirement that punishment be *deserved?*

3. An argument defending the fairness of "selective incapacitation" is developed in Note, Selective Incapacitation: Reducing Crime through Prediction of Recidivism, 96 Harv. L. Rev. 511 (1982). The author stresses, with respect to the problem of false positives, that "[a]n offender who would be mistakenly singled out by a selective incapacitation policy could easily receive an unnecessarily long sentence under the present informal consideration of these same factors." Id. at 529. Similarly, the author argues that the potentially invidious social and economic variables used in selective incapacitation proposals "are already used by both judges and parole boards in setting sentence lengths." Id. For an opposing view that develops ethical and empirical objections in depth, see Cohen, Selective Incapacitation: An Assessment, 1984 U. Ill. L. Rev. 253.

Chapter Four

Defining Criminal Conduct—The Elements of Just Punishment

Page 262. At the end of footnote a add:

See also Woozley, A Duty to Rescue: Some Thoughts on Criminal Liability, 69 Va. L. Rev. 1273 (1983).

Page 263. Before "Notes and Questions" add:

See J. C. Smith, Liability for Omissions in the Criminal Law, 4 Legal Stud. 88 (1984); Robinson, Criminal Liability for Omissions: A Brief Summary and Critique of the Law in the United States, 29 N.Y.L.S.L. Rev. 101 (1984).

Page 266. After the first excerpt and the reference to the Kennedy article, delete the discussion of the *Quinlan* case and insert:

BARBER v. SUPERIOR COURT

California District Court of Appeal
147 Cal. App. 3d 1006, 195 Cal. Rptr. 484 (1983)

[After a preliminary hearing, the magistrate dismissed murder and consipiracy charges against two physicians. The Superior Court set aside the magistrate's order and reinstated the complaint. The physicians then petitioned the Court of Appeal for review of the decision of the Superior Court.]

COMPTON, A. J. . . .

Deceased Clarence Herbert underwent surgery. . . . [W]hile in the recovery room, Mr. Herbert suffered a cardio-respiratory arrest. He was revived by a team of physicians and nurses and immediately placed on life support equipment.

Within the following three days, it was determined that Mr. Herbert was in a deeply comatose state.... [Tests] indicated that Mr. Herbert had suffered severe brain damage, leaving him in a vegetative state, which was likely to be permanent.

At that time petitioners [his physicians] informed Mr. Herbert's family of their opinion as to his condition and chances for recovery. While there is some dispute as to the precise terminology used by the doctors, it is clear that they communicated to the family that the prognosis for recovery was extremely poor. At that point, the family convened and drafted a written request to the hospital personnel stating that they wanted "all machines taken off that are sustaining life" (sic). As a result, petitioners, either directly or as a result of orders given by them, caused the respirator and other life-sustaining equipment to be removed. Mr. Herbert continued to breathe without the equipment but showed no signs of improvement.... After two more days had elapsed, petitioners, after consulting with the family, ordered removal of the intravenous tubes which provided hydration and nourishment. From that point until his death, Mr. Herbert received nursing care which preserved his dignity and provided a clean and hygienic environment.

The precise issue for determination by this court is whether the evidence presented before the magistrate was sufficient to support his determination that petitioners should not be held to answer to the charges of murder, and conspiracy to commit murder....

Murder is the *unlawful* killing of a human being,... with malice aforethought."...

...[W]e accept the superior court judge's analysis that if petitioners unlawfully and intentionally killed Mr. Herbert, the malice could be presumed regardless of their motive.

The use of the term "unlawful" in defining a criminal homicide is generally to distinguish a criminal homicide from those homicides which society has determined to be "justifiable" or "excusable." Euthanasia, of course, is neither justifiable nor excusable in California....

Historically, death has been defined in terms of cessation of heart and respiratory function. Health and Safety Code section 7180(a)(2) now provides for an alternative definition in terms of irreversible cessation of all brain function....

Of course it is conceded by all that at the time petitioners terminated further treatment, Mr. Herbert was not "dead" by either statutory or historical standards since there was still some minimal brain activity....

We thus turn to an analysis of the superior court's determination that petitioners' conduct was "unlawful" as a matter of law....

As a predicate to our analysis of whether the petitioners' conduct amounted to an "unlawful killing," we conclude that the cessation of "heroic" life support measures is not an affirmative act but rather a withdrawal or omission of further treatment.

Even though these life support devices are, to a degree, "self-propelled," each pulsation of the respirator or each drop of fluid introduced into the patient's body by intravenous feeding devices is comparable to a manually administered injection or item of medication. Hence "disconnecting" of the mechanical devices is comparable to withholding the manually administered injection or medication.

Further we view the use of an intravenous administration of nourishment and fluid, under the circumstances, as being the same as the use of the respirator or other form of life support equipment. . . .

Medical nutrition and hydration may not always provide net benefits to patients. Medical procedures to provide nutrition and hydration are more similar to other medical procedures than to typical human ways of providing nutrition and hydration. Their benefits and burdens ought to be evaluated in the same manner as any other medical procedure. . . .

There is no criminal liability for failure to act unless there is a legal duty to act. Thus the critical issue becomes one of determining the duties owed by a physician to a patient who has been reliably diagnosed as in a comatose state from which any meaningful recovery of cognitive brain function is exceedingly unlikely. . . .

A physician has no duty to continue treatment, once it has proved to be ineffective. Although there may be a duty to provide life-sustaining machinery in the *immediate* aftermath of a cardio-respiratory arrest, there is no duty to continue its use once it has become futile in the opinion of qualified medical personnel. . . .

Of course, the difficult determinations that must be made under these principles [are] the point at which further treatment will be of no reasonable benefit to the patient, who should have the power to make that decision and who should have the authority to direct termination of treatment.

No precise guidelines as to when or how these decisions should be made can be provided by this court since this determination is essentially a medical one to be made at a time and on the basis of facts which will be unique to each case. . . .

Several authorities have discussed the issue of which life-sustaining procedures must be used and for how long their use must be maintained in terms of "ordinary" and "extraordinary" means of treatment. The use of these terms begs the question. A more rational approach involves the determination of whether the proposed treatment is proportionate or disproportionate in terms of the benefits to be gained versus the burdens caused.

Under this approach, proportionate treatment is that which, in the view of the patient, has at least a reasonable chance of providing benefits to the patient, which benefits outweigh the burdens attendant to the treatment. . . . [A] treatment course which is only minimally painful or intrusive may nonetheless be considered disproportionate to the potential benefits if the prognosis is virtually hopeless for any significant improvement in condition.[a] . . .

Of course the patient's interests and desires are the key ingredients of the decision making process. . . .

When the patient, however, is incapable of deciding for himself, because of his medical condition or for other reasons, there is no clear authority on the issue of who and under what procedure is to make the final decision. . . .

Under the circumstances of this case, the wife was the proper person to act as a surrogate for the patient with the authority to decide issues regarding further treatment, and would have so qualified had judicial approval been sought. There is no evidence that there was any disagreement among the wife and children. Nor was there any evidence that they were motivated in their decision by anything other than love and concern for the dignity of their husband and father.

Furthermore, in the absence of legislative guidance, we find no legal requirement that prior judicial approval is necessary before any decision to withdraw treatment can be made. . . .

In summary we conclude that the petitioners' omission to continue treatment under the circumstances, though intentional and with knowledge that the patient would die, was not an unlawful failure to perform a legal duty. . . .

. . . The superior court erred in determining that as a matter of law the evidence required the magistrate to hold petitioners to answer. . . .

NOTE

For purposes of determining whether cessation of treatment (for example, by pulling an intravenous tube from the patient's arm) should be classified as an "act" or an "omission," should it be relevant to consider the reasons *why* the criminal law ordinarily punishes only for "acts"? In Leng, Death and the Criminal Law, 45 Mod. L. Rev. 206, 208-209 (1982), the author argues that "the act/omission distinction does not rest upon what is done, or upon a concept of willed muscular contraction, but upon the impact of what is done on the victim. . . .

a. What is, or should be, the meaning of the word *virtually* in this sentence? — EDS.

[T]ermination of [life] support is an omission . . . [because it] has no positive effect on the patient but merely fails to avert the natural cessation of vital functions." Contrast the reasons underlying the act requirement that are developed at Casebook pages 258-259. In terms of these reasons, is it plausible to characterize the pulling of an intravenous tube as an omission?

Suppose that the intravenous tube is pulled by an intruder who wants to watch the patient suffer. In terms of the analysis suggested by Professor Leng and by Professor Williams (Casebook pages 265-266), would we have to categorize the intruder's behavior as a mere "omission"?

Page 276. Before Note 3 add:

For a criticism of the Model Penal Code mens rea provisions on the ground that they fail to make a sufficient number of distinctions, see Robinson & Grall, Element Analysis in Defining Criminal Liability: The Model Penal Code and Beyond, 35 Stan. L. Rev. 681 (1983). Developments in the English courts are critically reviewed in Glazebrook, Case and Comment: Criminal Negligence, 43 Cambridge L.J. 1 (1984); Wells, The Mental Element in Crime, 1974-83: Lighthouse Some Good, [1984] Crim. L. Rev. 652.

Page 282. After line 5 insert:

PROBLEM

After being hired as an engineer by a company doing defense contracting work, Yermian filled out a personnel security form and provided false information about his job history and criminal record. Later he signed a typed version of the form, on the bottom of which was a warning that any false representation would be a violation of 18 U.S.C. §1001. The form was forwarded to the Defense Department for a security clearance investigation, and when Yermian's misrepresentations were discovered, he was prosecuted. Section 1001 provides that "[w]hoever, in any matter within the jurisdiction of any department or agency of the United States knowingly and willfully . . . makes any false . . . statements . . . shall be fined not more than $10,000 or imprisoned not more than five years, or both." Yermian admitted that he knew his statements were false but claimed that he had no knowledge that his statements were made in a matter within the jurisdiction of a federal agency. The trial court charged that the jury could convict if Yermian either knew or should have known of federal agency jurisdiction. Was this a correct interpretation of the statute? The U.S. Court of

Appeals for the Ninth Circuit reversed, 708 F.2d 365 (1983), but the Supreme Court reinstated the conviction. United States v. Yermian, 104 S. Ct. 2936 (1984). Writing for five Justices, Justice Powell said:

> The statute contains no language suggesting any additional element of intent, such as a requirement that false statements be "knowingly made in a matter within federal agency jurisdiction," or "with the intent to deceive the federal government." On its face, therefore, §1001 requires that the Government prove that false statements were made knowingly and willfully, and it unambiguously dispenses with any requirement that the Government also prove that those statements made with actual knowledge of federal agency jursidiction. . . . [T]he statutory language makes clear that Congress did not intend the terms "knowingly and willfully" to establish the standard of culpability for the jurisdictional element of §1001. The jurisdictional language appears in a phrase separate from the prohibited conduct modified by terms "knowingly and willfully."

In dissent, Justice Rehnquist (joined by Justices Brennan, Stevens and O'Connor) wrote:

> Notwithstanding the majority's repeated, but sparsely supported, assertions that the evidence of Congress' intent not to require actual knowledge is "convincing," and "unambiguous," I believe that the language and legislative history of §1001 can provide "no more than a guess as to what Congress intended.". . . . [T]he Court's reasoning here amounts to little more than simply pointing to the ambiguous phrases and proclaiming them clear. In my view, it is quite impossible to tell which phrases the terms "knowingly and willfully" modify, and the magic wand of ipse dixit does nothing to resolve that ambiguity. . . .
>
> Nor does the fact that the "in any matter" language appears as an introductory phrase at the beginning of the statute support the Court's conclusion that Congress did not intend that phrase to be modified by the culpability language. This is so because, before the 1948 revision of the statute—a housekeeping overhaul intended to make no substantive changes—the "in any matter" language in fact did *not* appear as an introductory phrase in the statute. Before the 1948 revision, the 1934 statute read as follows:
>
>> [W]hoever shall knowingly and willfully . . . make . . . any false or fraudulent statements or representations, . . . *in any matter within the jurisdiction of any department or agency of the United States* . . . shall be fined not more than $10,000 or imprisoned not more than ten years, or both.
>
> (emphasis added). . . .
>
> Seemingly aware of the broad range of conduct that §1001 could sweep within its scope under today's interpretation, the Court apparently does not hold that the words "in any matter within the jurisdiction of any department or agency of the United States" are jurisdictional words *only* and that *no* state of mind is required with respect to federal agency involvement. Instead, the Court suggests that some lesser state of mind may well be required in §1001

prosecutions in order to prevent the statute from becoming a "trap for the unwary." . . .

. . . I think that the Court's opinion will engender more confusion than it will resolve with respect to the culpability requirement in §1001 cases not before the Court.

Questions: How *should* the Court have interpreted §1001? What state of mind would be required to establish a violation of §1001 under the mens rea provisions of the Model Penal Code?

Note that in *Yermian,* the trial judge's instructions required at least negligence with respect to the element of federal agency jurisdiction. But given the Court's reasoning in *Yermian,* should §1001 be read to require any mens rea at all with respect to this element? One post-*Yermian* decision has held that the statute must now be read to make the existence of federal agency jurisdiction a matter of strict liability. United States v. Green, 36 Crim. L. Rptr. 2118 (9th Cir., Oct. 23, 1984).

The *Yermian* case should be considered again after examination of United States v. Feola, Casebook page 666. See this Supplement page 61, infra.

Page 286. Before Regina v. Morgan insert the following:

PEOPLE v. OLSEN

Supreme Court of California
36 Cal. 3d 638, 685 P.2d 52 (1984)

BIRD, C.J.

Is a reasonable mistake as to the victim's age a defense to a charge of lewd or lascivious conduct with a child under the age of 14 years (Pen. Code, §288, subd. (a)[1])?

In early June 1981, Shawn M. was 13 years and 10 months old. At that time, her parents were entertaining out-of-town guests. Since one of the visitors was using Shawn's bedroom, Shawn suggested that she sleep in her family's camper trailer which was parked in the driveway

---

1. Section 288, subdivision (a) provides in relevant part:

Any person who shall willfully and lewdly commit any lewd or lascivious act . . . upon or with the body, or any part or member thereof, of a child under the age of 14 years, with the intent of arousing, appealing to, or gratifying the lust or passions or sexual desires of such person or of such child, shall be guilty of a felony and shall be imprisoned in the state prison for a term of three, six, or eight years. . . .

in front of the house. Shawn's parents agreed to this arrangement on the condition that she keep the windows shut and the door locked. . . .

At trial, Shawn testified to the following events. On her third night in the trailer, she locked the door as instructed by her parents. She then fell asleep, but was awakened by appellant Olsen who was knocking on the window and asking to be let in. Shawn said nothing and appellant left. Approximately a half-hour later, Garcia came up to the window and asked if he could enter. Shawn did not respond so he left. . . . After both appellant and Garcia left, Shawn went to sleep.

Shawn was then awakened by the sound of barking dogs and by Garcia, who had a knife by her side and his hand over her mouth.[2] Garcia called to appellant to come in, and appellant entered the trailer.

Garcia told Shawn to let appellant "make love" to her, or he—Garcia—would stab her. . . .

. . . Appellant proceeded to have sexual intercourse with Shawn. . . . While appellant was still [doing so], her father entered the trailer. Mr. M. grabbed appellant as he was trying to leave, and Garcia stabbed Mr. M. in order to free appellant.

Shawn testified that she knew Garcia "pretty well." . . . She also testified that she was very good friends "off and on" with appellant and that during one three-month period she spent almost every day at appellant's house. At the time of the incident, however, Shawn considered Garcia her boyfriend.[3]

Finally, Shawn admitted that she told both Garcia and appellant that she was over 16 years old. She also conceded that she looked as if she were over 16.[4]

Garcia testified to quite a different set of events. . . . On . . . the day before the offense Shawn invited him to spend the night in the trailer with her so that they could have sex. He and Shawn engaged in sexual intercourse about four times that evening. Shawn invited Garcia to come back the following night at midnight.

The next night, after two unsuccessful attempts to enter the trailer, Garcia and appellant were told by Shawn to return at midnight. . . .

---

2. Although Shawn testified she locked the trailer door, she failed to explain how Garcia entered the trailer. A subsequent examination of the trailer revealed that there were no signs of a forced entry.

3. Shawn admitted that she had engaged in intercourse before the night of June 3rd, but denied having any such prior experience with either Garcia or appellant. However, she did admit having had sexual relations, short of intercourse, with both of them in the past.

4. Patricia Alvarez, a police officer, testified that appellant told her that he thought Shawn was 17.

Shawn, wearing only a pair of panties, opened the door and invited them in. She told them . . . that she wanted "to make love" with appellant first. When Mr. M. entered the trailer, appellant was on top of Shawn. Garcia denied threatening Shawn with a knife, taking her nightgown off, breaking into the trailer or forcing her to have sex with them.[5]

At the conclusion of the trial, the court found Garcia and appellant guilty of violating section 288, subdivision (a).[7] In reaching its decision, the court rejected defense counsel's argument that a good faith belief as to the age of the victim was a defense to the section 288 charge. Appellant was sentenced to the lower term of three years in state prison. This appeal followed. . . .

The language of section 288 is silent as to whether a good faith, reasonable mistake as to the victim's age constitutes a defense to a charge under that statute. . . .

Twenty years ago, this court in People v. Hernandez overruled established precedent, and held that an accused's good faith, reasonable belief that a victim was 18 years or more of age was a defense to a charge of statutory rape.[10] . . .

One Court of Appeal has declined to apply *Hernandez* in an analogous context. In People v. Lopez (1969) 271 Cal. App. 2d 754, 77 Cal. Rptr. 59, the court refused to recognize a reasonable mistake of age defense to a charge of offering or furnishing marijuana to a minor. The court noted that the act of furnishing marijuana is criminal regardless of the age of the recipient and that furnishing marijuana to a minor simply yields a greater punishment than when the substance is furnished to an adult. "[A] mistake of fact relating only to the gravity of an offense will not shield a deliberate offender from the full consequences of the wrong actually committed." (Ibid.)

. . . There exists a strong public policy to protect children of tender years. . . . [S]ection 288 was enacted for that very prupose. Further-

---

5. Appellant's sister corroborated Shawn's testimony that Shawn made daily visits to the Olsen home during a three-month period. She testified that during these visits Shawn and appellant would go into the latter's bedroom and close the door. On one occasion, appellant's sister saw the two in bed together. [Four other witnesses described similar episodes involving Shawn and either appellant or other boys.]

7. Garcia was also found guilty of assault with a deadly weapon with infliction of great bodily injury [in the assault on Mr. M.]. Both Garcia and appellant were found not guilty of burglary, forcible rape, and lewd or lascivious acts upon a child under the age of 14 by use of force.. . . .

10. One commentator believes that *Hernandez* marked a clear break from the "universally accepted view of the courts in this country." (Annot., Mistake or Lack of Information as to Victim's Age as Defense to Statutory Rape (1966) 8 A.L.R.3d 1100, 1102-1105, and cases cited.) The view that mistake of age is not a defense to a charge of stautory rape still prevails in the overwhelming majority of jurisdictions. (See ibid., and later cases (1983 pocket supp.) pp. 72-73.)

more, even the *Hernandez* court recognized this important policy when it made clear that it did not contemplate applying the mistake of age defense in cases where the victim is of "tender years." . . .

This conclusion is supported by the Legislature's enactment of section 1203.066. Subdivision (a)(3) of that statute renders certain individuals convicted of lewd or lascivious conduct who "honestly and reasonably believed the victim was 14 years old or older" eligible for probation. The Legislature's enactment of section 1203.066, subdivision (a)(3). . . . strongly indicates that the Legislature did not intend such a defense to a section 288 charge. To recognize such a defense would render section 1203.066, subdivision (a)(3) a nullity, since the question of probation for individuals who had entertained an honest and reasonable belief in the victim's age would never arise. . . .

Other legislative provisions also support the holding that a reasonable mistake of age is not a defense to a section 288 charge. Time and again, the Legislature has recognized that persons under 14 years of age are in need of special protection. . . .

The Legislature has also determined that persons who commit sexual offenses on children under the age of 14 should be punished more severely than those who commit such offenses on children under the age of 18. . . .

It is significant that a violation of section 288 carries a much harsher penalty than does unlawful sexual intercourse (§261.5), the crime involved in *Hernandez*. Section 261.5 carries a maximum punishment of one year in the county jail or three years in state prison, while section 288 carries a maximum penalty of eight years in state prison. The different penalties for these two offenses further supports the view that there exists a strong public policy to protect children under 14. . . .

The legislative purpose of section 288 would not be served by recognizing a defense of reasonable mistake of age. . . . Accordingly, the judgment of conviction is affirmed.

GRODIN, J., concurring and dissenting.

I agree that the enactment of Penal Code section 1203.066, which renders eligible for probation persons convicted of lewd or lascivious conduct who "honestly and reasonably believed the victim was 14 years old or older" is persuasive evidence that in the eyes of the Legislature such a belief is not a defense to the crime.[1] What troubles me is the

---

1. I do not agree that legislative intent to eliminate good faith mistake of fact as a defense can be inferred from the imposition of relatively higher penalties for that crime. On the contrary, as this court has stated in connection with the crime of bigamy: "The severe penalty imposed . . . the serious loss of reputation conviction entails, the infre-

notion that a person who acted with such belief, and is not otherwise shown to be guilty of any criminal conduct,[2] may not only be convicted but be sentenced to prison notwithstanding his eligibility for probation when it appears that his belief did not accord with reality. To me, that smacks of cruel or unusual punishment.

. . . I recognize . . . that our legal system includes certain "strict liability" crimes, but generally these are confined to the so-called "regulatory" or "public welfare" offenses. . . . (Morissette v. United States (1952) 342 U.S. 246). Moreover, with respect to such crimes, *"The accused, if he does not will the violation, usually is in a position to prevent it with no more care than society might reasonably expect . . . from one who assumed his responsibilities. Also, penalties commonly are relatively small, and conviction does no grave damage to an offender's reputation."* (Id., at p. 256, emphasis added.)

Even in the regulatory context, "judicial and academic acceptance of liability without fault has not been enthusiastic." (Jeffries & Stephan, Defenses, Presumptions, and Burden of Proof in the Criminal Law (1979) 88 Yale L.J. 1325, 1373.) And 'with respect to traditional crimes, it is a widely accepted normative principle that conviction should not be had without proof of fault. At least when the offense carries serious sanctions and the stigma of official condemnation, liability should be reserved for persons whose blameworthiness has been established." (Id., at pp. 1373-1374)

. . . No doubt the standard of what is reasonable must be set relatively high in order to accomplish the legislative objective of protecting persons under 14 years of age against certain conduct. Perhaps it is not enough that a person "looks" to be more than 14; perhaps there is a duty of reasonable inquiry besides. At some point, however, the belief becomes reasonable by any legitimate standard, so that one would say the defendant is acting in a way which is no different from the way our society would expect a reasonable, careful, and law-abiding citizen to act.

At that point, it seems to me, the imposition of criminal sanctions, particularly imprisonment, simply cannot be tolerated in a civilized society. . . .

---

quency of the offense, and the fact that it has been regarded . . . as a crime involving moral turpitude, make it extremely unlikely that the Legislature meant to include the morally innocent to make sure the guilty did not escape." (People v. Vogel (1956) 46 Cal. 2d 798, 804, 299 P.2d 850.)

2. The People suggest that defendant was at least guilty of "sexual intercourse accomplished with a female not the wife of the perpetrator, where the female is under the age of 18 years." Defendant was neither charged nor convicted of that offense, however, and it is by no means clear from the record that he had sexual intercourse with the victim.

Page 292. At the bottom of the page add:

NOTE

The English courts continue to struggle with the question whether, or when, a mistake of fact can exculpate if it is not based on reasonable grounds. For a helpful summary of the decisions, see Cowley, The Retreat from *Morgan*, [1982] Crim. L. Rev. 200. The author argues that although *Morgan* seemingly required a subjective mens rea as a matter of general principles and was not limited to the context of rape, subsequent decisions in other contexts appear to have returned to the *Tolson* approach, under which a mistake is generally a defense only if reasonable.

Page 296. Before "c. Mistake of Law" insert:

For thought-provoking development of the argument that the defendant who makes an unreasonable mistake as to consent exhibits sufficient moral culpability to be held guilty of rape, see Temkin, The Limits of Reckless Rape, [1983] Crim. L. Rev. 5; Wells, Swatting the Subjectivist Bug, [1982] Crim. L. Rev. 209.

Page 304. Before Hopkins v. State add:

REGINA v. TAAFFE, [1983] 2 All E.R. 625 (Ct. App.): The appellant drove a car into the green lane of the ferry terminal at Sheerness and told the customs officer who was on duty there that he had nothing to declare. The car was searched . . . and inside were found to be five packages containing cannabis resin. Not unnaturally the search then moved to the body of the appellant himself, and strapped to his back and underneath his clothing were discovered three further packages also containing cannabis resin, the total quantity being that stated in the indictment.

The appellant was cautioned by the customs officer and was asked if he knew what the substances in the packages were. He replied, "No, I am waiting to find out, because if it is drugs . . . " and there his reply ended. So the officer then asked him, "What did you think was in the packages?" And to that he replied simply, "Money."

. . . The question is this: on the assumption that the following facts are established, has the alleged offence been committed? . . . (1) the appellant was enlisted by a third party in Holland to import a substance from that country into England in fraudulent evasion of the prohibition upon its importation and he did so import it; (2) that substance was in fact cannabis, the importation of which is prohibited by the Misuse of Drugs Act 1971; (3) the appellant mistakenly believed the substance to be currency; (4) currency is not subject to any such prohibition; (5) the appellant mistakenly believed that currency was the subject of a prohibition against importation. . . .

One starts with the premise that this is not an offence of absolute liability. It is plain, from the use of the word "knowingly" in section 170(2)[a] that the prosecution have the task of proving the existence of mens rea, the mental element of guilt. Mens rea in this context means the mental element required by the particular statute on the part of the defendant before the prosecution can succeed.

What then in this case was the relevant mental element which section 170(2) required to be proved? It seems to us that it was primarily knowledge that the substance which was being imported was a drug, or certainly was a substance of some sort the importation of which was prohibited. . . .

What then if the jury in the present case had been asked to decide the matter and had come to the conclusion that the appellant might have believed that what he was importing was currency and not prohibited drugs? He is to be judged against the facts that he believed them to be. Had this indeed been currency and not cannabis, no offence would have been committed. Does it make any difference that the appellant thought wrongly that by clandestinely importing currency he was committing an offence? Mr. Aylwin [for the prosecution] strongly submits that it does. He suggests that a man in this situation has to be judged according to the total mistake that he has made, both the mistake with regard to the fact of what he was carrying and also [the] mistake of law as to the effect of carrying that substance. We think that submission is wrong. It no doubt made his actions morally reprehensible. It did not, in our judgment, turn what he, for the purpose of argument, believed to be the importation of currency into the commission of a criminal offence. His views on the law as to the importation of currency were to that extent, in our judgment, irrelevant. . . .

[F]or the reasons we have endeavoured to give, this appeal must be followed and the conviction quashed.[b]

---

a. Customs and Excise Management Act 1979, s.170(2): "if any person is, in relation to any goods, in any way knowingly concerned in any fraudulent evasion . . . (b) of any prohibition . . . in force with respect to the goods . . . he shall be guilty of an offense. . . ."

b. The decision of the Court of Appeal was affirmed by the House of Lords. [1984] 2 Weekly L. Rep. 326.

LIPAROTA v. UNITED STATES

Supreme Court of the United States
37 Crim. L. Rptr. 3042 (May 13, 1985)

BRENNAN, J., delivered the opinion of the Court.

The federal statute governing food stamp fraud provides that "whoever knowingly uses, transfers, acquires, alters, or possesses coupons or authorization cards in any manner not authorized by [the statute] or the regulations" is subject to a fine and imprisonment. 7 U.S.C. §2024(b).[1] The question presented is whether in a prosecution under this provision the Government must prove that the defendant knew that he was acting in a manner not authorized by statute or regulations.

Petitioner Frank Liparota was the co-owner with his brother of Moon's Sandwich Shop in Chicago, Illionis. He was indicted for acquiring and possessing food stamps in violation of §2024(b). The Department of Agriculture had not authorized petitioner's restaurant to accept food stamps. At trial, the Government proved that petitioner on three occasions purchased food stamps from an undercover Department of Agriculture agent for substantially less than their face value. On the first occasion, the agent informed petitioner that she had $195 worth of food stamps to sell. The agent then accepted petitioner's offer of $150 and consummated the transaction in a back room of the restaurant with petitioner's brother. A similar transaction occurred one week later, in which the agent sold $500 worth of coupons for $350. Approximately one month later, petitioner bought $500 worth of food stamps from the agent for $300.

In submitting the case to the jury, the District Court rejected petitioner's proposed "specific intent" instruction, which would have instructed the jury that the Government must prove that "the defendant knowingly did an act which the law forbids, purposely intending to violate the law." Concluding that "[t]his is not a specific intent crime" but rather a "knowledge case," the District Court instead instructed the jury as follows:

> When the word "knowingly" is used in these instructions, it means that the Defendant realized what he was doing, and was aware of the nature of his conduct, and did not act through ignorance, mistake, or accident. Knowledge may be proved by defendant's conduct and by all of the facts and circumstances surrounding the case.

. . . Petitioner objected that this instruction required the jury to find merely that he knew that he was acquiring or possessing food stamps;

1. The statute provides in relevant part: "[W]hoever knowingly uses, transfers, acquires, alters, or possesses coupons or authorization cards in any manner not authorized, by this chapter or the regulations issued pursuant to this chapter shall, if such coupons or authorization cards are of a value of $100 or more, be guilty of a felony. . . ."

he argued that the statute should be construed instead to reach only "people who knew that they were acting unlawfully." The judge did not alter or supplement his instructions, and the jury returned a verdict of guilty.

Petitioner appealed his conviction to the Court of Appeals for the Seventh Circuit. . . . The Court of Appeals rejected petitioner's arguments. . . .

Absent indication of contrary purpose in the language or legislative history of the statute, we believe that §2024(b) requires a showing that the defendant knew his conduct to be unauthorized by statute or regulations.[9] "The contention that an injury can amount to a crime only when inflicted by intention is no provincial or transient notion. It is as universal and persistent in mature systems of law as belief in freedom of the human will and a consequent ability and duty of the normal individual to choose between good and evil." Morissette v. United States, [342 U.S. 246, 250 (1952), Casebook, p. 324]. Thus, in United States v. United States Gypsum Co., 438 U.S. 422, 438 (1978), we noted that "[c]ertaintly far more than the simple omission of the appropriate phrase from the statutory definition is necessary to justify dispensing with an intent requirement" and that criminal offenses requiring no mens rea have a "generally disfavored status." Similarly, in this case, the failure of Congress explicitly and unambiguously to indicate whether mens rea is required does not signal a departure from this background assumption of our criminal law.

This construction is particularly appropriate where, as here, to interpret the statute otherwise would be to criminalize a broad range of apparently innocent conduct. For instance, §2024(b) declares it criminal to use, transfer, acquire, alter, or possess food stamps in any manner not authorized by statute or regulations. The statute provides further that "[c]oupons issued to eligible households shall be used by them only to

9. The Dissent repeatedly claims that our holding today creates a defense of "mistake of law." Our holding today no more creates a "mistake of law" defense than does a statute making knowing receipt of stolen goods unlawful. In both cases, there is a legal element in the definition of the offense. In the case of a receipt of stolen goods statute, the legal element is that the goods were stolen; in this case, the legal element is that the "use, transfer, acquisition," etc. were in a manner not authorized by statute or regulations. It is not a defense to a charge of receipt of stolen goods that one did not know that such receipt was illegal, and it is not a defense to a charge of a §2024(b) violation that one did not know that possessing food stamps in a manner unauthorized by statute or regulations was illegal. It *is*, however, a defense to a charge of knowing receipt of stolen goods that one did not know that the goods were stolen, just as it is a defense to a charge of a §2024(b) violation that one did not know that one's possession was unauthorized. See American Law Institute, Model Penal Code §2.02, Comment 11, p. 131 (Tentative Draft No. 4, 1955); United States v. Freed, 401 U.S. 601, 614-615 (1971) (Brennan, J., concurring). Cf. United States v. Morissette, 342 U.S. 246 (1952) (holding that it is a defense to a charge of "knowingly converting" federal property that one did not know that one was doing was a conversion).

purchase food in retail food stores which have been approved for participation in the food stamp program *at prices prevailing in such stores.*" 7 U.S.C. §2016(b) (emphasis added); see also 7 CFR §274.10(a) (1984). This seems to be the *only* authorized use. A strict reading of the statute with no knowledge of illegality requirement would thus render criminal a food stamp recipient who, for example, used stamps to purchase food from a store that, unknown to him, charged higher than normal prices to food stamp program participants. Such a reading would also render criminal a nonrecipient of food stamps who "possessed" stamps because he was mistakenly sent them through the mail due to administrative error, "altered" them by tearing them up, and "transferred" them by throwing them away. Of course, Congress *could* have intended that this broad range of conduct be made illegal, perhaps with the understanding that prosecutors would exercise their discretion to avoid such harsh results. However, given the paucity of material suggesting that Congress did so intend, we are reluctant to adopt such a sweeping interpretation. . . .

The Government advances two additional arguments in support of its reading of the statute. First, the Government contends that this Court's decision last Term in United States v. Yermian, 468 U. S.— (1984) [this Supplement p. 25 supra], supports its interpretation. *Yermian* involved a prosecution for violation of the federal false statement statute, 18 U.S.C. §1001. All parties agreed that the statute required proof at least that the defendant "knowingly and willfully" made a false statement. Thus, unlike the instant case, all parties in *Yermian* agreed that the Government had to prove the defendant's mens rea. . . . In contrast, the Government in the instant case argues that no mens rea is required with respect to any element of the crime. Finally, *Yermian* found that the statutory language was unambiguous and that the legislative history supported its interpretation. The statute at issue in this case differs in both respects.

Second, the Government contends that the §2024(b) offense is a "public welfare" offense, which the Court defined in United States v. Morissette, 342 U.S., at 252-253, to "depend on no mental element but consist only of forbidden acts or omissions." Yet the offense at issue here differs substantially from those "public welfare offenses" we have previously recognized. In most previous instances, Congress has rendered criminal a type of conduct that a reasonable person should know is subject to stringent public regulation and may seriously threaten the community's health or safety. Thus, in United States v. Freed, 401 U.S. 601 (1971), we examined the federal statute making it illegal to receive or possess an unregistered firearm. In holding that the Government did not have to prove that the recipient of unregistered hand grenades knew that they were unregistered, we noted that "one would hardly be surprised to learn that possession of hand grenades is not an innocent act." See also United States v. International Minerals & Chemical Corp., 402 U.S. 558, 564-565 (1971). Similarly, in United States v. Dotterweich, 320 U.S. 277, 284 (1943), the Court held that a corporate officer could violate the Food and Drug Act when his firm shipped adulterated and misbranded drugs, even "though consciousness of wrongdoing be totally wanting." See also United States v. Balint, 258 U.S. 250 (1922). The distinctions between these cases and the instant case are clear. A food stamp can hardly be compared to a hand grenade, see *Freed,* nor can the unauthorized acquisiton or possession of food stamps be compared to the selling of adulterated drugs, as in *Dotterweich.*

We hold that in a prosecution for violaton of §2024(b), the Government must prove that the defendant knew that his acquisition or possession of food stamps was in a manner unauthorized by statute or regulations. This holding does not put an unduly heavy burden on the Government in prosecuting violators of §2024(b). To prove that petitioner knew that his acquisition or possession of food stamps was unauthorized, for example, the Government need not show that he had knowledge of specific regulations governing food stamp acquisition or possession. . . . Rather, as in any other criminal prosecution requiring mens rea, the Government may prove by reference to facts and circumstances surrounding the case that petitioner knew that his conduct was unauthorized or illegal.[17]

Reversed.

WHITE, J., with whom THE CHIEF JUSTICE joins, dissenting. . . .

The Court views the statutory problem here as being how far down the sentence the term "knowingly" travels. Accepting for the moment that if "knowingly" does extend to the "in any manner" language today's holding would be correct—a position with which I take issue below—I doubt that it gets that far. The "in any manner" language is separated from the litany of verbs to which "knowingly" is directly connected by the intervening nouns. We considered an identically phrased statute last Term in United States v. Yermian, 468 U. S.— (1984). . . . We found that under the "most natural reading" of the

---

17. In this case, for instance, the Government introduced evidence that petitioner bought food stamps at a substantial discount from face value and that he conducted part of the transaction in a back room of his restaurant to avoid the presence of the other patrons. Moreover, the Government asserts that food stamps themselves are stamped "nontransferable." A jury could have inferred from this evidence that petitioner knew that his acquisition and possession of the stamps was unauthorized.

statute, "knowingly and willfully" applied only to the making of false or fraudulent statements and not to the fact of jurisdiction. By the same token, the "most natural reading" of §2024(b) is that knowingly modifies only the verbs to which it is attached.[1]

In any event, I think that the premise of this approach is mistaken. Even accepting that "knowingly" does extend through the sentence, or at least that we should read §2024(b) as if it does, the statute does not mean what the Court says it does. Rather, it requires only that the defendant be aware of the relevant aspects of his conduct. A requirement that the defendant know that he is acting in a particular manner, coupled with the fact that that manner is forbidden, does not establish a defense of ignorance of the law. It creates only a defense of ignorance or mistake of fact. Knowingly to do something that is unauthorized by law is not the same as doing something knowing that it is unauthorized by law.

This point is demonstrated by the hypothetical statute referred to by the majority, which punishes one who "knowingly sells a security without a permit." Even if "knowingly" does reach "without a permit," I would think that a defendant who knew that he did not have a permit, though not that a permit was required, could be convicted.

Section 2024(b) is an identical statute, except that instead of detailing the various legal requirements, it incorporates them by proscribing use of coupons "in any manner not authorized" by law. This shorthand approach to drafting does not transform knowledge of illegality into an element of the crime. As written, §2024(b) is substantively no different than if it had been broken down into a collection of specific provisions making crimes of particular improper uses. . . .

The Court's opinion provides another illustration of the general point: someone who used food stamps to purchase groceries at inflated prices without realizing he was overcharged. I agree that such a person may not be convicted, but not for the reason given by the majority. The purchaser did not "knowingly" use the stamps in the proscribed manner, for he was unaware of the circumstances of the transaction that made it illegal.

1. The majority's efforts to distinguish *Yermian* are unavailaing. First, it points out that under the statute at issue there, the prosecution had to establish some mens rea because it had to show a knowing falsehood. However, as the majority itself points out elsewhere, different mental states can apply to different elements of an offense. The fact that in *Yermian* mens rea had to be proved as to the first element was irrelevant to the Court's holding that it did not with regard to the second. There is no reason to read this statute differently. Second, the majority states that the language in *Yermian* was "unambiguous." Since it is identical, the language at issue in this case can be no less so. Finally, the majority notes that the Court in *Yermian* did not decide whether the prosecution might have to prove that the defendant "should have known" that his statements were within the agency's jurisdiction. However, that passing statement was irrelevant to the interpretation of the statute's language the Court did undertake.

The majority and I would part company in result as well as rationale if the purchaser knew he was charged higher than normal prices but not that overcharging is prohibited. In such a case, he would have been aware of the nature of his actions, and therefore the purchase would have been "knowing." I would hold that such a mental state satisfied the statute. Under the Court's holding, as I understand it, that person could not be convicted because he did not know that his conduct was illegal. . . .

The broad principles of the Court's opinion are easy to live with in a case such as this. But the application of its reasoning might not always be so benign. For example, §2024(b) is little different from the basic federal prohibition on the manufacture and distribution of controlled substances. 21 U.S.C. §841(a) provides:

> Except as authorized by this subchapter, it shall be unlawful for any person knowingly or intentionally—
> (1) to manufacture, distribute, or dispense, or possess with intent to manufacture, distribute or dispense, a controlled substance. . . . .

I am sure that the members of the majority would agree that a defendant charged under this provision could not defend on the ground that he did not realize his manufacture was unauthorized or that the particular substance was controlled. See United States v. Balint, 285 U.S. 250 (1922). . . . By the same token, I think, someone in petitioner's position should not be heard to say that he did not know his purchase of food stamps was unauthorized, though he may certainly argue that he did not know he was buying food stamps. . . . [T]he logic of the Court's opinion would require knowledge of illegality for conviction under any statute making it a crime to do something "in any manner not authorized by law" or "unlawfully." . . .

In relying on the "background assumption of our criminal law" that mens rea is required, the Court ignores the equally well-founded assumption that ignorance of the law is no excuse. It is "the conventional position that knowledge of the existence, meaning or application of the law determining the elements of an offense is not an element of that offense. . . ." Model Penal Code [§2.02, Comment at 130 (Tent. Draft No. 4, 1955)].

This Court's prior cases indicate that a statutory requirement of a "knowing violation" does not supersede this principle. For example, under the statute at issue in United States v. International Minerals & Chemical Corp., 402 U.S. 558 (1971), the Interstate Commerce Commission was authorized to promulgate regulations regarding the transportation of corrosive liquids, and it was a crime to "knowingly violat[e] any such regulation." Viewing the word "regulations" as "a shorthand designation for specific acts or omissions which violate the Act," we adhered to the traditional rule that ignorance of the law is not a defense. The violation had to be "knowing" in that the defendant had to know that he was transporting corrosive liquids and not, for example, merely water. But there was no requirement that he be aware that he was violating a particular regulation. Similarly, in this case the phrase "in any manner not authorized by" the statute or regulations is a shorthand incorporation of a variety of legal requirements. To be convicted, a defendant must have been aware of what he was doing, but not that it was illegal. . . .

. . . This reading does not abandon the "background assumption" of mens rea by creating a strict liability offense, and is consistent with the equally important background assumption that ignorance of the law is not a defense.

I wholly agree that "[t]he contention that an injury can amount to a crime only when inflicted by intention is no provincial or transient notion." Morissette v. United States, 342 U.S. 246, 250 (1952). But the holding of the court below is not at all inconsistent with that longstanding and important principle. Petitioner's conduct was intentional; the jury found that petitioner "realized what he was doing, and was aware of the nature of his conduct, and did not act through ignorance, mistake, or accident." Whether he knew which regulation he violated is beside the point.

QUESTIONS

Are the *International Minerals* and *Liparota* decisions consistent with one another? If not, which result is preferable?

How should the two cases be analyzed under the principles of Model Penal Code §§2.02(9), 2.04(1)?

Page 350. Before "Section D. Legality" insert:

SOLEM v. HELM

Supreme Court of the United States
103 S. Ct. 3001 (1983)

POWELL, J., delivered the opinion of the Court.

The issue presented is whether the Eighth Amendment proscribes a life sentence without possibility of parole for a seventh nonviolent felony.

I

By 1975 the State of South Dakota had convicted respondent Jerry Helm of six nonviolent felonies. In 1964, 1966, and 1969 Helm was convicted of third-degree burglary. In 1972 he was convicted of obtaining money under false pretenses. In 1973 he was convicted of grand larceny. And in 1975 he was convicted of third-offense driving while intoxicated. The record contains no details about the circumstances of any of these offenses, except that they were all nonviolent, none was a crime against a person, and alcohol was a contributing factor in each case.

In 1979 Helm was charged with uttering a "no account" check for $100. The only details we have of the crime are those given by Helm to the state trial court:

> "I was working in Sioux Falls, and got my check that day, was drinking and I ended up here in Rapid City with more money than I had when I started. I knew I'd done something I didn't know exactly what. If I would have known this, I would have picked the check up. I was drinking and didn't remember, stopped several places."

After offering this explanation, Helm pleaded guilty.

Ordinarily the maximum punishment for uttering a "no account" check would have been five years imprisonment in the state penitentiary and a $5,000 fine. As a result of his criminal record, however, Helm was subject to South Dakota's recidivist statute:

> When a defendant has been convicted of at least three prior convictions [sic] in addition to the principal felony, the sentence for the principal felony shall be enhanced to the sentence for a Class 1 felony.

The maximum penalty for a "Class 1 felony" was life imprisonment in the state penitentiary and a $25,000 fine. Moreover, South Dakota law explicitly provides that parole is unavailable.... The Governor is authorized to pardon prisoners, or to commute their sentences, but no other relief from sentence is available even to a rehabilitated prisoner.

Immediately after accepting Helm's guilty plea, the South Dakota Circuit Court sentenced Helm to life imprisonment under §22-7-8. The court explained:

> "I think you certainly earned this sentence and certainly proven that you're an habitual criminal and the record would indicate that you're beyond rehabilitation and that the only prudent thing to do is to lock you up for the rest of your natural life, so you won't have further victims of your crimes, just be coming back before Courts. You'll have plenty of time to think this one over."

The South Dakota Supreme Court, in a 3-2 decision, affirmed the sentence despite Helm's argument that it violated the Eighth Amendment.

After Helm had served two years in the state penitentiary, he requested the Governor to commute his sentence to a fixed term of years.... The Governor denied Helm's request....

In November 1981, Helm sought habeas relief in the United States

District Court for the District of South Dakota. . . . Although the District Court recognized that the sentence was harsh, it concluded that this Court's recent decision in Rummel v. Estelle, 445 U.S. 263 (1980), was dispositive. It therefore denied the writ.

The United States Court of Appeals for the Eighth Circuit reversed. . . .

We granted certiorari. . . .

II

The Eighth Amendment declares: "Excessive bail shall not be required, nor excessive fines imposed, nor cruel and unusual punishments inflicted." The final clause prohibits not only barbaric punishments, but also sentences that are disproportionte to the crime committed.

The principle that a punishment should be proportionate to the crime is deeply rooted and frequently repeated in common-law jurisprudence. . . .

The constitutional principle of proportionality has been recognized explicitly in this Court for almost a century. . . .

There is no basis for the State's assertion that the general principle of proportionality does not apply to felony prison sentences. The constitutional language itself suggests no exception for imprisonment. We have recognized that the Eighth Amendment imposes "parallel limitations" on bail, fines, and other punishments, and the text is explicit that bail and fines may not be excessive. It would be anomalous indeed if the lesser punishment of a fine and the greater punishment of death were both subject to proportionality analysis, but the intermediate punishment of imprisonment were not. There is also no historical support for such an exception. . . . And our prior cases have recognized explicitly that prison sentences are subject to proportionality analysis. . . .

In sum, we hold as a matter of principle that a criminal sentence must be proportionate to the crime for which the defendant has been convicted. Reviewing courts, of course, should grant substantial deference to the broad authority that legislatures necessarily possess in determining the types and limits of punishments for crimes, as well as to the discretion that trial courts possess in sentencing convicted criminals. But no penalty is per se constitutional. As the Court noted in Robinson v. California, 370 U.S. [660, 667 (1962)], a single day in prison may be unconstitutional in some circumstances.

Second, it may be helpful to compare the sentences imposed on other criminals in the same jurisdiction. If more serious crimes are subject to the same penalty, or to less serious penalties, that is some indication that the punishment at issue may be excessive. . . .

Third, courts may find it useful to compare the sentences imposed for commission of the same crime in other jurisdictions. . . .

Application of these factors assumes that courts are competent to judge the gravity of an offense, at least on a relative scale. In a broad sense this assumption is justified, and courts traditionally have made these judgments—just as legislatures must make them in the first instance. Comparisons can be made in light of the harm caused or threatened to the victim or society, and the culpability of the offender. Thus in Enmund [v. Florida, 102 S. Ct. 3368 (1982), this Supplement page 56 infra] the Court determined that the petitioner's conduct was not as serious as his accomplices' conduct. Indeed, there are widely shared views as to the relative seriousness of crimes. See Rossi, Waite, Bose & Berk, The Seriousness of Crimes: Normative Structure and Individual Differences, 39 Am. Soc. Rev. 224, 237 (1974). For example, as the criminal laws make clear, nonviolent crimes are less serious than crimes marked by violence or the threat of voilence.

. . . The absolute magnitude of the crime may be relevant. . . . It also is generally recognized that attempts are less serious than completed crimes. See, e.g., S.D. Codified Laws §22-4-1 (1979); 4 Blackstone *15. . . .

Turning to the culpability of the offender, there are again clear distinctions that courts may recognize and apply. . . . Most would agree that negligent conduct is less serious than intentional conduct. . . .

. . . [Thus,] there are generally accepted criteria for comparing the severity of different crimes on a broad scale, despite the difficulties courts face in attempting to draw distinctions between similar crimes. . . .

IV

It remains to apply the analytical framework established by our prior decisions to the case before us. We first consider the relevant criteria, viewing Helm's sentence as life imprisonment without possibility of parole. We then consider the State's argument that the possibility of commutation is sufficient to save an otherwise unconstitutional sentence.

Helm's crime was "one of the most passive felonies a person could commit." State v. Helm, 287 N.W.2d, at 501 (Henderson, J., dissenting). It involved neither violence nor threat of violence to any person. The $100 face value of Helm's "no account" check was not trivial, but neither was it a large amount. One hundred dollars was less than half the amount South Dakota required for a felonious theft. It is easy to see why such a crime is viewed by society as among the less serious offenses.

Helm, of course, was not charged simply with uttering a "no account" check, but also with being an habitual offender.[21] And a State is justified in punishing a recidivist more severely than it punishes a first offender. Helm's status, however, cannot be considered in the abstract. His prior offenses, although classified as felonies, were all relatively minor. All were nonviolent and none was a crime against a person. Indeed, there was no minimum amount in either the burglary or the false pretenses statutes, and the minimum amount covered by the grand larceny statute was fairly small.

Helm's present sentence is life imprisonment without possibility of parole. Barring executive clemency, see infra, Helm will spend the rest of his life in the state penitentiary. This sentence is far more severe than the life sentence we considered in Rummel v. Estelle. Rummel was likely to have been eligible for parole within 12 years of his initial confinement, a fact on which the Court relied heavily. Helm's sentence is the most severe punishment that the State could have imposed on any criminal for any crime. Only capital punishment, a penalty not authorized in South Dakota when Helm was sentenced, exceeds it.

We next consider the sentences that could be imposed on other criminals in the same jurisdiction. . . .

In sum, there were a handful of crimes that were necessarily punished by life imprisonment: murder, and, on a second or third offense, treason, first degree manslaughter, first degree arson, and kidnapping. There was a larger group for which life imprisonment was authorized in the discretion of the sentencing judge, including: treason, first degree manslaughter, first degree arson, and kidnapping; attempted murder, placing an explosive device on an aircraft, and first degree rape on a second or third offense; and any felony after three prior offenses. Finally, there was a large group of very serious offenses for which life imprisonment was not authorized, including a third offense of heroin dealing or aggravated assault. . . .

Finally, we compare the sentences imposed for commission of the same crime in other jurisdictions. The Court of Appeals found that "Helm could have received a life sentence without parole for his offense in only one other state, Nevada." . . . . But even under Nevada law, a life sentence without possibility of parole is merely authorized in

---

21. We must focus on the principal felony—the felony that triggers the life sentence—since Helm already has paid the penalty for each of his prior offenses. But we recognize, of course, that Helm's prior convictions are relevant to the sentencing decision.

these circumstances. We are not advised that any defendant such as Helm, whose prior offenses were so minor, actually has received the maximum penalty in Nevada. . . .

The State argues that the present case is essentially the same as Rummel v. Estelle, for the possibility of parole in that case is matched by the possibility of executive clemency here. . . .

As a matter of law, parole and commutation are different concepts, despite some surface similarities. Parole is a regular part of the rehabilitative process. Assuming good behavior, it is the normal expectation in the vast majority of cases. The law generally specifies when a prisoner will be eligible to be considered for parole, and details the standards and procedures applicable at that time. See, e.g., Greenholz v. Nebraska Penal Inmates, 442 U.S. 1 (1979) [Casebook page 1088]; Morrissey v. Brewer, 408 U.S. 471, 477 (1972) [Casebook page 1076]. Thus it is possible to predict, at least to some extent, when parole might be granted. Commutation, on the other hand, is an ad hoc exercise of executive clemency. A Governor may commute a sentence at any time for any reason without reference to any standards. See, e.g., Connecticut Board of Pardons v. Dumschat, 452 U.S. 458 (1981) [Casebook page 1093]. . . .

In South Dakota commutation is more difficult to obtain than parole. . . . In fact, no life sentence has been commuted in over eight years, while parole—where authorized—has been granted regularly during that period. . . .

The possibility of commutation is nothing more than a hope for "an ad hoc exercise of clemency." It is little different from the possibility of executive clemency that exists in every case in which a defendant challenges his sentence under the Eighth Amendment. Recognition of such a bare possibility would make judicial review under the Eighth Amendment meaningless.

V

. . . Applying objective criteria, we find that Helm has received the penultimate sentence for relatively minor criminal conduct. . . . We conclude that his sentence is significantly disproportionate to his crime, and is therefore prohibited by the Eighth Amendment. The judgment of the Court of Appeals is accordingly affirmed.

BURGER, C.J., with whom WHITE, REHNQUIST, and O'CONNOR, JJ., join, dissenting.

The controlling law governing this case is crystal clear, but today the Court blithely discards any concept of stare decisis, trespasses gravely

on the authority of the States, and distorts the concept of proportionality of punishment by tearing it from its moorings in capital cases. Only
two Terms ago, we held in Rummel v. Estelle, 445 U.S. 263 (1980), that
a life sentence imposed after only a *third* nonviolent felony conviction
did not constitute cruel and unusual punishment under the Eighth
Amendment. Today, the Court ignores its recent precedent and holds
that a life sentence imposed after a *seventh* felony conviction constitutes
cruel and unusual punishment under the Eighth Amendment. Moreover, I reject the fiction that all Helm's crimes were innocuous or
nonviolent. Among his felonies were three burglaries and a third conviction for drunk driving. By comparison Rummel was a relatively "model citizen." Although today's holding cannot rationally be reconciled
with *Rummel*, the Court does not purport to overrule *Rummel*. I therefore dissent.

The Court's starting premise is that the Eighth Amendment's Cruel
and Unusual Punishments Clause "prohibits not only barbaric punishments, but also sentences that are disproportionate to the crime committed." What the Court means is that a sentence is unconstitutional if
it is more severe than five justices think appropriate. In short, all sentences of imprisonment are subject to appellate scrutiny the ensure that
they are "proportional" to the crime committed. . . .

The *Rummel* Court categorically rejected the very analysis adopted by
the Court today. Rummel had argued that various objective criteria
existed by which the Court could determine whether his life sentence
was proportional to his crimes. In rejecting Rummel's contentions, the
Court explained why each was insufficient to allow it to determine in
an *objective* manner whether a given sentence of imprisonment is proportionate to the crime for which it is imposed.

. . . Today's conclusion by five Justices that they are able to say that
one offense has less "gravity" than another is nothing other than a
bald substitution of individual subjective moral values for those of the
legislature. . . .

The simple truth is that "[n]o neutral principle of adjudication permits a federal court to hold that in a given situation individual crimes
are too trivial in relation to the punishment imposed." . . . Legislatures
are far better equipped than we are to balance the competing penal
and public interests and to draw the essentially arbitrary lines between
appropriate sentences for different crimes.

By asserting the power to review sentences of imprisonment for ex-
cessiveness the Court launches into uncharted and unchartable waters.
Today it holds that a sentence of life imprisonment, without the possibility of parole, is excessive punishment for a seventh allegedly "nonviolent" felony. How about the eighth "nonviolent" felony? The ninth?

The twelfth? Suppose one offense was a simple assult? Or selling liquor to a minor? Or statutory rape? Or price-fixing? The permutations are endless and the Court's opinion is bankrupt of realistic guiding principles. Instead, it casually lists several allegedly "objective" factors and arbitrarily asserts that they show respondent's sentence to be "significantly disproportionate" to his crimes. . . . I can see no limiting principle in the Court's holding.

The differences between this case and *Rummel* are insubstantial. First, Rummel committed three truly nonviolent felonies, while respondent, as noted at the outset, committed seven felonies, four of which cannot fairly be characterized as "nonviolent." At the very least, respondent's burglaries and his third-offense drunk driving posed real risk of serious harm to others. It is sheer fortuity that the places respondent burglarized were unoccupied and that he killed no pedestrians while behind the wheel. What would have happened if a guard had been on duty during the burglaries is a matter of speculation, but the possibilities shatter the notion that respondent's crimes were innocuous, inconsequential, minor, or "nonviolent." Four of respondent's crimes, I repeat, had harsh potentialities for violence. Respondent, far more than Rummel, has demonstrated his inability to bring his conduct into conformity with the minimum standards of civilized society. Clearly, this difference demolishes any semblance of logic in the Court's conclusion that respondent's sentence constitutes cruel and unusual punishment although Rummel's did not.

The Court's opinion necessarily reduces to the proposition that a sentence of life imprisonment with the possibility of commutation, but without possibility of parole, is so much more severe than a life sentence with the possibility of parole that one is excessive while the other is not. This distinction does not withstand scrutiny. . . .

. . . In South Dakota, the historical evidence shows that since 1964, 22 life sentences have been commuted to terms of years, while requests for commutation of 25 life sentences were denied. And, of course, those requests for commutation may be renewed.

. . . The Court would do well to heed Justice Black's comments about judges overruling the considered actions of legislatures under the guise of constitutional interpretation:

> Such unbounded authority in any group of politically appointed or elected judges would unquestionably be sufficient to classify our Nation as a government of men, not the government of laws of which we boast. With a "shock the conscience" test of constitutionality, citizens must guess what is the law, guess what a majority of nine judges will believe fair and reasonable. Such a test wilfully throws away the certainty and security that lies in a written constitution, one that does not alter with a judge's health, belief, or his politics.

Boddie v. Connecticut, 401 U.S. 371, 393 (1971) (Black, J., dissenting).

Page 361. Before Nash v. United States insert:

See also Jeffries, Legality, Vagueness and the Construction of Penal Statutes, 71 Va. L. Rev. 189 (1985).

Page 370. After the first paragraph of the Note add:

In Kolender v. Lawson, 103 S. Ct. 1855 (1983), the Supreme Court held void for vagueness a California statute that required persons who loiter or wander on the streets to provide a "credible and reliable" identification and to account for their presence, when requested to do so by a police officer under circumstances that "indicate to a reasonable man that the public safety demands such identification." Speaking for the Court, Justice O'Connor wrote that the statute, as construed by the California courts, provided no standard for determining what a suspect must do to satisfy its requirements and therefore vested virtually complete discretion in the hands of the police. Justices White and Rehnquist dissented.

Several courts have considered the effect of *Kolender* on loitering statutes closely patterned on the Model Penal Code formulation. In both Watts v. State, 463 So. 2d 205 (Fla. 1985), and Porta v. Mayor, City of Omaha, 593 F. Supp. 863 (D. Neb. 1984), courts distinguished the California provision involved in *Kolender* and upheld statutes comparable to Model Penal Code §250.6. Both courts reasoned that the loitering provisions at issue gave a suspected person the "opportunity" to justify his or her presence but did not require the person to do so and did not make the refusal to answer in itself an element of the offense; rather the refusal to identify is only one of several circumstances that the officer may consider in determining whether the circumstances warrant concern for the public safety. Query: Does this reasoning suggest that the Code provision is substantially narrower than the statute involved in *Kolender,* or does the Code provision in effect vest the police officer with even broader discretion?

Chapter Five

Rape

Page 391. At the bottom of the page add the following additional Note:

3. *Other judicial approaches.* Although the great majority of jurisdictions apparently still retain the marital exemption, many courts continue to question that exemption. In People v. Liberta, 64 N.Y.2d 152, 474 N.E.2d 567 (1984), the defendant, who was living apart from his wife pursuant to a Family Court protection order, brutally forced her to submit to intercourse and was prosecuted for rape. The New York Court of Appeals found that "there is no rational basis for distinguishing between marital rape and non-marital rape," 474 N.E.2d, at 573, and accordingly ruled New York's statutory marital exemption unconstitutional and upheld the rape conviction. Under *Liberta* a husband apparently can be prosecuted for rape whether or not the parties are living apart at the time of the incident in question. See also Commonwealth v. Chretien, 383 Mass. 123, 417 N.E.2d 1203 (1981); State v. Rider, 449 So. 2d 903 (Fla. App. 1984). But see People v. Brown, 632 P.2d 1025 (Colo. 1981).

A narrower approach is taken in Weishaupt v. Commonwealth, 227 Va. 389, 315 S.E.2d 847 (1984). The court there held that a husband charged with rape cannot invoke the marital exemption when the wife has "conduct[ed] herself in a manner that establishes a de facto end to the marriage." (In *Weishaupt* the wife had moved out of the common home, and the parties had been separated for 11 months at the time of the offense). But in Kizer v. Commonwealth, 321 S.E.2d 291 (Va. 1984), a rape conviction based on a violent sexual assault was nonetheless reversed. In that case the husband had moved to separate quarters, the parties had not engaged in sexual intercourse for more than six months, and the husband had filed for custody of the child. However, because the wife had at various points made attempts to make the marriage "work" and because she had hesitated to file for divorce, the court found that her "vacillating" conduct was too equivocal to establish that the husband knew or should have known that she considered the marriage at an end.

Page 395. Before "2. Special jury instructions" insert:

Although the District of Columbia courts have abandoned the corroboration requirement when the alleged rape victim is a "mature" female, corroboration is still required when the victim is "immature." See, e.g., Fitzgerald v. United States, 443 A.2d 1295 (D.C. App. 1982) (corroboration required where complainant was 12-year-old).

Page 402. After second paragraph of the Note add:

For a discussion of the effect of Rule 412 of the Federal Rules of Evidence on the admissibility of evidence of the victim's prior sexual behavior, see Annot., 65 A.L.R. Fed. 519 (1983).

Chapter Six
Homicide

Page 448. After the Salmond excerpt add:

A federal panel, appointed by the U.S. Department of Transportation to study the costs and benefits of retaining the national 55 MPH speed limit, estimated that raising the speed limit to 65 MPH would cause an additional 500 deaths per year. The panel also estimated that under the higher speed limit 850,000 hours of travel time would be saved for every life lost. N.Y. Times, Nov. 28, 1984, p.A16. Questions: Is enactment of the higher speed limit justifiable? Should motorists who drive at 65 MPH (in violation of a posted speed limit) have a good defense against a charge of criminal negligence?

Page 457. At the end of Note 5(c) add:

The House of Lords has taken some controversial positions on these issues in recent years. See Ashall, Manslaughter — The Impact of *Caldwell*, [1984] Crim. L. Rev. 467; Williams, Recklessness and Intention Again, 2 Legal Stud. 189 (1982); Spencer, Manslaugter by Gross Negligence — Return to Victorian Values, [1983] Cambridge L.J. 187.

Page 462. Before Note 5 insert:

Most American courts continue to hold that extreme carelessness in the operation of an automobile can support a conviction of murder — on the theory that the defendant had an actual awareness of a great risk of fatal harm. E.g., People v. Watson, 30 Cal. 3d 290, 637 P.2d 279 (1981). For contrary view, see Essex v. Commonwealth, 322 S.E.2d 216 (Va. 1984).

Page 482. Delete the second paragraph and substitute:

PEOPLE v. DILLON, 34 Cal. 3d 441, 668 P.2d 697 (1983): [Defendant, a 17-year-old high school student, knew that marijuana was growing on a well-guarded, quarter-acre section of a nearby farm. Armed with shotguns and other weapons, the defendant and several classmates approached the farm and spread out through its fields in a plan to take the marijuana, by force if necessary. When the defendant saw one of the farm owners coming toward him with a shotgun, he shot and killed the owner. Defendant was convicted of first-degree murder, on the theory that the killing occurred in the course of an attempted robbery. After holding that both "standing crops" and contraband can be the subject of robbery, the California Supreme Court went on to consider the application of the felony-murder rule:]

. . . [O]ur opinions make it clear we hold no brief for the felony-murder rule. We have repeatedly stated that the felony murder is a "highly artificial concept" which "deserves no extension beyond its required application." . . .

Nevertheless, a thorough review of legislative history convinces us that in California — in distinction to Michigan — the first degree felony-murder rule is a creature of statute. However much we may agree with the reasoning of *Aaron*, therefore, we cannot duplicate its solution to the problem: this court does not sit as a super-legislature with the power to judicially abrogate a statute merely because it is unwise or outdated. . . .

[The Michigan] statute is a copy of the first legislation in the nation on this topic, enacted in Pennsylvania in 1794, and . . . it has long been construed by Michigan courts to be no more than a degree-fixing device, i.e, . . . when a "murder" is otherwise proved — to wit, an unlawful killing with malice aforethought — the statute simply fixes the degree thereof at first degree if it was committed by one of the listed means or during one of the listed felonies; it does not automatically transform all killings so committed into first degree murder.[9]

From the reported history of the 1794 Pennsylvania statute it clearly appears the *Aaron* court was correct in characterizing it as a degree-fixing measure rather than a codification of the common law felony-murder rule. California has a very similar statute, Penal Code section 189, and we need not speculate on its provenance; its draftsmen acknowledged that it was taken directly from the 1794 Pennsylvania statute. . . .

At this point, however, our law appears to diverge sharply from that of Pennsylvania and Michigan. . . .

. . . [A]lthough the balance remains close, we hold that the evidence of present legislative intent . . . is sufficient to outweigh the contrary implications of the language of section 189 and its predecessors. We

9. The [*Aaron*] opinion notes that the 1794 Pennsylvania statute is so construed by the Pennsylvania courts and that similar statutes in other jurisdictions are likewise viewed only as degree-fixing measures.

are therefore required to construe section 189 as a statutory enactment of the first degree felony-murder rule in California.

[The court then went on to hold, however, that because first-degree felony murder encompasses a wide range of culpability — from accidental to deliberate, premeditated killings — the court had to consider whether the first-degree penalty, life imprisonment, was disproportionate to the culpability of the defendant in the particular case. Applying such decisions as In re Lynch, Case page 345, Solem v. Helm, this Supplement page 40 supra, and Enmund v. Florida, this Supplement page 56 infra, the Court found that with respect to the defendant, "an unusually immature youth [who] had no prior trouble with the law," 34 Cal. 3d at 488, the first-degree penalty constituted cruel and unusual punishment. In conclusion, the court held:]

. . . Nevertheless, because he intentionally killed the victim without legally adequate provocation, defendant may and ought to be punished as a second degree murderer.

The judgment . . . is modified by reducing the degree of the crime to murder in the second degree and, as so modified, is affirmed.

Questions: Has the California court really reaffirmed the felony-murder rule? How does the result under the *Dillon* approach differ from the result under the approach of *Aaron?* Which approach is preferable?

Page 487. Before subsection (iii) insert:

6. If a drug dealer sells cocaine or heroin and a purchaser dies of a self-injected overdose, can the dealer be convicted of murder on a felony-murder theory? In Heacock v. Commonwealth, 323 S.E.2d 90 (Va. 1984), the court so held, noting that cocaine had been classified as a controlled substance because of its "high potential for abuse." But for a contrary conclusion, see State v. Randolph, 676 S.W.2d 943 (Tenn. 1984). The court there held:

> We decline to adopt a general rule that death occurring during or resulting from the commission of any felony shall automatically be deemed murder in the second degree regardless of the nature of the offense proscribed. . . . [D]eath is neither the inevitable nor necessarily the most probable result of the injection of a controlled substance. . . . However, when all the circumstances shown in this record are taken into account [defendant had been warned that the heroin was dangerous and should not be sold until it had been "cut"], we are of the opinion that, if competently established beyond a

reasonable doubt, they could justify a conclusion by the trier of fact that
appellant and his co-defendants acted with such conscious indifference to
the consequences . . . as to evince malice.

Note that even if the mens rea of murder is established in such a case,
there is room for debate about whether the drug dealer's actions can be
considered the proximate cause of death. See Problem, Casebook page
552.

Page 498. Before Note 2 insert:

Suppose that police officers enter a house to arrest marijuana dealers
consummating a sale. After the principals are arrested, a police officer
searching the house is shot and killed by a co-felon attempting to evade
arrest. Are the dealers who had already been arrested responsible for
the killing on a felony-murder theory, or are they relieved of liability
on the ground that the arrest terminated their participation? In State v.
Amaro, 436 So. 2d 1056 (Fla. App. 1983), the court upheld the convictions, finding that the co-felon's act was foreseeable and in furtherance
of the common design. Query: What result if some of the felons had
been taken to jail before the shooting took place?

Page 505. Before Note 2 insert:

REGINA v. PAGETT, 76 Crim. App. Rep. 279 (1983): [When police
officers came to defendant's flat to arrest him for a series of violent
offenses, defendant grabbed a 16-year-old girl, held her in front of his
body as a shield, and began firing at the officers. The officers returned
his fire and as a result the girl was killed. Convicted of murder, the
defendant argues on that appeal that] where the act which immediately
resulted in fatal injury was the act of another party, albeit in legitimate
self-defence, then the ensuing death was too remote or indirect to be
imputed to the original agressor. . . .

The United States authorities cited to us, which reflect some diversity
of judicial opinion, were concerned with the question whether an accused person could be convicted of the murder or manslaughter of a
person by shooting, where the fatal shot was fired not by the accused
but by some other person. In Commonwealth v. Almeida, (1949) 362
Pa. 596, a case concerned with a robbery in the course of which shots
were exchanged with police officers and a police officer was killed, the
accused (one of the robbers) was convicted of the murder of the police
officer. It was held by the Supreme Court of Pennsylvania. . . . "The
felonious acts of the robbers in firing shots at the policeman, well
knowing that their fire would be returned, as it should have been, was

(sic) the proximate cause of Officer Ingling's death." The point was, as appears from this brief quotation, considered by the court to raise a question of causation. The decision was subsequently followed in Commonwealth v. Thomas (1955) 382 Pa. 639, 117 A.2d 204. However, in Commonwealth v. Redline (1958) 137 A.2d 472, the earlier case of *Thomas* was overruled, and *Almeida* itself, although not formally overruled, was plainly disapproved by the majority of the court. . . .

Examination of the reasoning of the majority of the court in *Redline* (supra) shows, however, that the decision provides no useful guidance to an English court today. The point is that the reasoning of the Pennsylvanian court was concerned with the scope of the felony murder doctrine which, since the abolition of constructive malice in murder by section 1 of the Homicide Act 1957, forms no part of English law. The approach of the majority of the Pennsylvanian court is amply illustrated by the following passage . . . : "In adjudging a felony-murder, it is to be remembered at all times that the thing which is imputed to a felon for a killing incidental to his felony is *malice* and *not the act of killing*. . . . [I]n order to convict for felony-murder, *the killing must have been done by the defendant or by an accomplice or confederate or by one acting in furtherance of the felonious undertaking.*" It was this principle, reflected in the earlier cases, which was reaffirmed in the case of Commonwealth v. Redline (supra).

It at once becomes apparent that the case of *Redline*, and the earlier cases cited in it in support of the conclusion in that case, are of no assistance to an English court concerned with the English law of murder, of which the felony-murder doctrine forms no part. Even so, it was pressed upon us by Lord Gifford [counsel for the defense] that there either was, or should be, a comparable rule of English law, whereby, as a matter of policy, no man should be convicted of homicide (or, we imagine, any crime of violence to another person) unless he himself, or another person acting in concert with him, fired the shot (or, we imagine, struck the blow) which was the immediate cause of the victim's death (or injury).

. . . So far as we are aware, there is no such rule in English law; and, in the absence of any doctrine of constructive malice, we can see no basis in principle for any such rule in English law. Lord Gifford urged upon us that, in a case where the accused did not, for example, fire the shot which was the immediate cause of the victim's death, he will inevitably have committed some lesser crime, and that it would be sufficient that he should be convicted of that lesser crime. So, on the facts of the present case, it would be enough that the appellant was convicted of the crime of attempted murder of the two police officers. . . . We see no force in this submission. In point of fact, it is not difficult to imagine circumstances in which it would manifestly be inadequate for the accused merely to be convicted of a lesser offence. . . .

In our judgment, the question whether an accused person can be held guilty of homicide, either murder or manslaughter, of a victim the immediate cause of whose death is the act of another person must be determined on the ordinary principles of causation, uninhibited by any such rule of policy as that for which Lord Gifford has contended. . . .

[The court's discussion of those principles is reproduced in this Supplement page 59 infra.]

Page 518. At the bottom of the page add:

Detailed statistical studies now indicate that murder defendants who kill white victims are significantly more likely to receive the death penalty than murder defendants who kill black victims. See especially Baldus, Pulaski & Woodworth, Comparative Review of Death Sentences: An Empirical Study of the Georgia Experience, 74 J. Crim. L. & C. 661 (1983); Pulley v. Harris, 104 S. Ct. 871, 877-888 (1984) (Brennan, J., dissenting). To date, the courts have held such studies insufficient to establish that capital punishment violates either the equal protection guarantee or the prohibition against cruel and unusual punishment. In McCleskey v. Kemp, 753 F.2d 877 (11th Cir. 1985), the en banc Court of Appeals held that evidence of racially disparate impact cannot establish a constitutional violation in the absence of proof that the disparity results from a deliberate *intention* to discriminate on grounds of race; three judges dissented.

Page 529. Delete footnote 9, and after the last paragraph of text insert:

In Enmund v. Florida, 102 S. Ct. 3368 (1982), the evidence suggested that the defendant had waited in a getaway car while two accomplices approached a rural farmhouse and then robbed and murdered the elderly couple who lived there. The defendant was convicted of capital murder and sentenced to death, on the theory that the felony-murder rule and the Florida law of aiding and abetting made Enmund responsible for the lethal acts of his co-felons. The Supreme Court held that the Eighth Amendment prohibits imposition of the death penalty on a defendant "who does not himself kill, attempt to kill, or intend that a killing take place or that lethal force will be employed." Id. at 3376-3377. In an opinion by Justice White, the Court stressed that Enmund's culpability was "plainly different from that of the robbers who killed" and that it is "fundamental that causing harm intentionally must be punished more severely than causing the same harm unintentionally." Id. at 3377, quoting H. L. A. Hart, Punishment and Responsibility 162 (1968). Chief Justice Burger and Justices Powell, Rehnquist, and O'Connor dissented.

Enmund apparently poses no barrier to imposition of the death penalty on an accomplice who actually intended to kill and participated in the preparations for the killing. See State v. Tison, 142 Ariz. 446, 690 P.2d 747 (1984).[a] Query: What result if the state seeks to impose the death penalty on a robber who commits the actual killing, but who does not have (or cannot be proved to have) an intention to kill?

a. For a provocative account of this case, see A. Dershowitz, The Best Defense 289-318 (1982).

Chapter Seven

The Significance of Resulting Harm

Page 535. Before Stephenson v. State insert:

REGINA v. PAGETT

Court of Criminal Appeal, 1983
76 Crim. App. Rep. 279

[In this case, other aspects of which are considered in this Supplement page 54 supra, the defendant held a girl in front of his body as a shield while he fired at officers attempting to arrest him. The officers returned his fire and as a result the girl was killed. The defendant argued that his own acts were not the proximate cause of death. Addressing this argument, the court referred to the discussion in H. L. A. Hart & A. Honore, Causation in the Law (1958), and continued as follows:]

. . . [T]he learned authors consider the circumstances in which the intervention of a third person, not acting in concert with the accused, may have the effect of relieving the accused of criminal responsibility. The criterion which they suggest should be applied in such circumstances is whether the intervention is voluntary, i.e. whether it is "free, deliberate and informed." We resist the temptation of expressing the judicial opinion whether we find ourselves in complete agreement with that definition; though we certainly consider it to be broadly correct and supported by authority. Among the examples which the authors give of non-voluntary conduct, which is not effective to relieve the accused of responsibility, are two which are germane to the present case, viz. a reasonable act performed for the purpose of self-preservation, and an act done in performance of a legal duty.

There can, we consider, be no doubt that a reasonable act performed for the purpose of self-preservation, being of course itself an act caused by the accused's own act, does not operate as a *novus actus interveniens*. If authority is needed for this almost self-evident proposition, it is to be found in such cases as *Pitts* (1842) C. & M. 284, and *Curley* (1909) 2 Cr. Ap. R. 96. In both these cases, the act performed for the purpose of self-preservation consisted of an act by the victim in attempting to escape from the violence of the accused, which in fact resulted in the victim's death. In each case it was held as a matter of law that, if the victim acted in a reasonable attempt to escape the violence of the accused, the death of the victim was caused by the act of the accused. Now one form of self-preservation is self-defence; for present purposes, we can see no distinction in principle between an attempt to escape the consequences of the accused's act, and a response which takes the form of self-defence. Furthermore, in our judgment, if a reasonable act of self-defence against the act of the accused causes the death of a third party, we can see no reason in principle why the act of self-defence, being an involuntary act caused by the act of the accused, should relieve the accused from criminal responsibility for the death of the third party. Of course, it does not necessarily follow that the accused will be guilty of the murder, or even of the manslaughter, of the third party; though in the majority of cases he is likely to be guilty at least of manslaughter. Whether he is guilty of murder or manslaughter will depend upon the question whether all the ingredients of the relevant offence have been proved; in particular, on a charge of murder, it will be necessary that the accused had the necessary intent. . . .

Chapter Eight
Group Criminality

Page 613. After the first paragraph insert:

For an effort to present a theory of accomplice liability that addresses most of the issues raised in the sections that follow, see Kadish, Complicity, Cause and Blame — An Essay in the Interpretation of Doctrine, 73 Calif. L. Rev. 602 (1985).

Page 635. Delete the last line of note 1, and substitute:

§5.01(3).

Page 659. After Note 2 insert the following new note:

3. In the course of delivering three kilograms of cocaine to undercover federal agents at a Miami motel, two drug dealers became suspicious, shooting erupted, and one of the dealers killed one of the federal agents. Several co-conspirators arrested outside the motel were convicted of the murder of the federal agent. On appeal the government conceded that the killing was not an intended object of the cocaine distribution ring but claimed that the outcome, though obviously "unexpected," was nonetheless "reasonably foreseeable" within the meaning of the *Pinkerton* doctrine. What result? See United States v. Alvarez, 37 Crim. L. Rptr. 2025 (11th Cir., March 20, 1985).

Page 673. Before Note 1 insert the following new note:

1a. With respect to the Court's interpretation of §111, reconsider the *Yermian* case, this Supplement page 25 supra. Under the false statements statute involved in *Yermian*, is the presence of federal agency jurisdiction a matter that is "jurisdictional only"? Or is federal agency jurisdiction a matter that is, in terms of Model Penal Code §1.13(10), connected with "the harm or evil . . . sought to be prevented by the law defining the offense"? If the latter, then what is the Court's justification for not requiring knowledge (or at least recklessness) with respect to the element of federal agency jurisdiction?

Page 714. Before the heading "4. Parties" insert:

For further discussion of the implications of *Elliott*, see Tarlow, RICO: The New Darling of the Prosecutor's Nursery, 49 Fordham L. Rev. 165, 243-257 (1980).

The holding in *Elliott* was significantly qualified by United States v. Sutherland, 656 F.2d 1181 (5th Cir. 1981). In *Sutherland* one defendant was a traffic court judge, and each of the other two (Walker and Maynard) was a person allegedly involved with the judge in a scheme to fix traffic tickets. The government conceded that neither Walker nor Maynard knew of the other's activities; under pre-RICO law there would have been two separate conspiracies — a "wheel" without a "rim." But the government claimed that the affairs of the traffic court constituted the RICO "enterprise" and that the three defendants could be charged with a single "enterprise conspiracy" under RICO. In essence, the government argued that "so long as the object of each conspiracy is participation in the same enterprise in violation of RICO, it matters not that the different conspiracies are otherwise unrelated." 656 F.2d at 1191. The Fifth Circuit conceded that some of the language in *Elliott* lent support to this argument, but noted that *Elliott* was addressed primarily to the problem that under prior law, it was difficult to infer a single agreement from the commission of highly diverse crimes. *Elliott* explained that "RICO helps to eliminate this problem by creating a substantive offense which ties together these diverse parties and crimes." The court then clarified the limitations on the holding in *Elliott* (656 F.2d at 1192-1194):

> *Elliott* does indeed hold that on the facts of that case a series of agreements that under pre-RICO law would constitute multiple conspiracies could under RICO be tried as a single "enterprise" conspiracy. But the language of *Elliott* explains that what ties these conspiracies together is not the mere fact that they involve the same enterprise, but is instead — as in any other conspiracy — an "agreement on an overall objective." What RICO does is to provide a new criminal objective by defining a new substantive crime. In *Elliott*, as here, that crime consists of participation in an enterprise through a pattern of racketeering activity. . . .
>
> To be sure, the government did not prove in *Elliott* that each of the conspirators had explicitly agreed with all of the others to violate the substantive RICO provision at issue. However, the government did prove that, as in a traditional "chain" conspiracy, the nature of the scheme was such that each defendant must necessarily have known that others were also conspiring to participate in the same enterprise through a pattern of racketeering activity. . . .
>
> . . . *Elliott* does not stand for the proposition that multiple conspiracies

may be tried on a single "enterprise conspiracy" count under RICO merely because the various conspiracies involve the same enterprise. What *Elliott* does state is two-fold: (1) a pattern of agreements that absent RICO would constitute multiple conspiracies may be joined under a single RICO conspiracy count if the defendants have agreed to commit a substantive RICO offense; and (2) such an agreement to violate RICO may, as in the case of a traditional "chain" or "wheel" conspiracy, be established on circumstantial evidence, i.e., evidence that the nature of the conspiracy is such that each defendant must necessarily have known that others were also conspiring to violate RICO.

In this case the government has not attempted to prove that Walker and Maynard agreed with each other to participate in a bribery scheme with Sutherland, nor has it contended that the nature of each defendant's agreement with Sutherland was such that he or she must necessarily have known that others were also conspiring to commit racketeering offenses in the conduct of the Municipal Court. We must conclude, therefore, that the multiple conspiracy doctrine precluded the joint trial of the two multiple conspiracies involved in this case on a single RICO conspiracy count. . . .

Page 720. After Note 2 add:

3. The unilateral approach to conspiracy has been rejected in Illinois. That state, like Indiana, has recently adopted a conspiracy statute patterned on the Model Penal Code. The Illinois provision states that "a person commits conspiracy when, with intent that an offense be committed, he agrees with another to the commission of that offense." Ill. Rev. Stat. 1981, ch. 28, par. 8-2(a). In a case involving a feigned accomplice, the Illinois Supreme Court held that the required "agree[ment]" could not exist unless at least two parties genuinely intended to carry out the plan. Rejecting the reasoning of the *Garcia* case, Casebook page 717, the Court said: "We doubt . . . that the drafters could have intended what represents a rather profound change in the law of conspiracy without mentioning it in the comments to section 8-2." People v. Foster, 99 Ill. 2d 48, 457 N.E.2d 405, 407 (1983). The court noted, however, that the Illinois solicitation statute would (like the corresponding Model Penal Code provision) "embrace virtually every situation in which one could be convicted of conspiracy under the unilateral theory." Id., 457 N.E.2d at 408.

Chapter Nine
Exculpation

Page 728. Before Note 1 insert the following additional Note:

1a. On remand in *Ibn-Tamas*, the trial court again excluded the expert testimony; it held that the defendant had failed to establish general scientific acceptance of Dr. Walker's methodology and accordingly that the prerequisites for the admissibility of expert testimony had not been satisfied. On appeal the court of appeals held that exclusion of the testimony was not improper under these circumstances. 455 A.2d 893 (D.C. App. 1983).

Page 728. At the end of the first paragraph of Note 1 insert:

Helpful comments on the problem include Mackinnon, Book Review, 34 Stan. L. Rev. 703 (1982) (reviewing A. Jones, Women Who Kill (1980)); Schneider, Equal Rights to Trial for Women: Sex Bias in the Law of Self-Defense, 15 Harv. C.R.-C.L.L. Rev. 623 (1980); Note, Partially Determined Imperfect Self-Defense: The Battered Wife Kills and Tells Why, 34 Stan. L. Rev. 615 (1982); Note, The Battered Spouse Syndrome as a Defense to a Homicide Charge under the Pennsylvania Crimes Code, 26 Vill. L. Rev. 105 (1980).

A thorough exploration of the "battered spouse" issue appears in State v. Kelly, 478 A.2d 364 (N.J. 1984). In that case defendant testified that her husband, in a drunken state, angrily argued with her, knocked her to the ground, and began choking her in the street. Two men separated them, and Mrs. Kelly moved away to find her daughter in the crowd. Shortly afterward, she observed her husband running toward her with his hands raised. Unsure whether he was armed, defendant pulled a pair of scissors from her purse and inflicted stab wounds that proved fatal. The prosecution presented testimony to show that Mrs. Kelly provoked the initial scuffle; that when separated from her husband and restrained by bystanders, she stated that she intended to kill him; and that she then chased him, caught up with him, and stabbed him with the scissors. The New Jersey

Supreme Court held that "battered spouse" testimony excluded at trial was relevant both to defendant's general credibility and to the reasonableness of her claimed belief that she was in imminent danger of death or serious injury. The court explained (478 A.2d at 377-378):

> The crucial issue of fact on which this expert's testimony would bear is why, given such allegedly severe and constant beatings, combined with threats to kill, defendant had not long ago left decedent. . . .
>
> The difficulty with the expert's testimony is that it *sounds* as if an expert is giving knowledge to a jury about something the jury knows as well as anyone else, namely, the reasonableness of a person's fear of imminent serious danger. That is not at all, however, what this testimony is *directly* aimed at. It is aimed at an area where . . . jurors' logic, drawn from their own experience, may lead to a wholly incorrect conclusion. . . . After hearing the expert, instead of saying Gladys Kelly could not have been beaten up so badly for if she had, she certainly would have left, the jury could conclude that her failure to leave was very much part and parcel of her life as a battered wife. The jury could conclude that instead of casting doubt on the accuracy of her testimony about the severity and frequency of prior beatings, her failure to leave actually reinforced her credibility.
>
> . . . [T]he expert's testimony might also enable the jury to find that the battered wife, because of the prior beatings, numerous beatings, as often as once a week, for seven years, from the day they were married to the day he died, is particularly able to predict accurately the likely extent of violence in any attack on her. That conclusion could significantly affect the jury's evaluation of the reasonableness of defendant's fear for her life.

The court remanded for a new trial but left it open to the prosecution to argue for exclusion of the evidence, despite its relevance, by questioning whether the methodology used by the expert has a sufficient scientific basis to produce uniform, reasonably reliable results.

Page 729. Before Note 3 insert:

2a. *Problem.* After a violent argument with his teenaged son, a father left to take the mother out to dinner. The son made careful preparations to shoot the father on his return. He waited in the darkened garage, armed with a 12-gauge shotgun, and when his father drove up and approached the garage door, the son opened fire and killed him. Should the son be permitted to introduce evidence showing that the father had subjected him to years of physical abuse? Should expert testimony concerning the psychological effects of such abuse be admissible in support of the son's claim of self-defense?

The Wyoming Supreme Court, relying on the *Buhrle* decision (Casebook pages 728-729), held this "battered child" evidence inadmissible. Jahnke v. State, 682 P.2d 991 (Wyo. 1984). One concurring judge wrote (682 P.2d at 1010): "This is a textbook case of first-degree murder. . . . In his defense, appellant employed the oldest, most common and most successful tactic in homicide cases. He put the deceased on trial. . . . There was no one to speak for the deceased. . . . [But by] no stretch of the imagination was this a case of self-defense." Two dissenting judges argued that admission of the battered child evidence was essential to permit the jury to understand whether the defendant could perceive himself in imminent danger and whether his response was that of a reasonable person similarly situated.

Page 730. After the second sentence of Note 4 insert:

The Criminal Division of the Court of Appeal has now held that a belief in the need to use defensive force need not be reasonable. Regina v. Williams, reported and commented on in [1984] Crim. L. Rev. 163.

Page 735. Before Note 4 insert:

One recent commentator has sharply challenged the prevailing doctrines that attempt to confine the use of deadly force within narrow bounds. In La Fond, The Case for Liberalizing the Use of Deadly Force in Self-Defense, 6 U. Puget Sound L. Rev. 237 (1983), the author criticizes cases like *Wanrow* (Casebook page 722) on the ground that they reverse convictions on artificial, formalistic grounds without confronting the real source of the difficulty — namely, the rule that deadly force can be used only to counter a threat of death or great bodily harm. Because this rule leaves many law-abiding citizens without a practically effective means of defense against an unlawful, nondeadly assault by an unpredictable or much stronger attacker, Professor La Fond proposes that resort to deadly force be permissible whenever it is "necessary to protect [the defendant] effectively" against a threat of unlawful physical violence. Id. at 280.

Page 742. Before Problem 2 insert:

Several recent decisions have adopted the view that one is obliged to retreat from one's own dwelling when the assailant is another occupant. See, e.g., State v. Bobbitt, 415 So. 2d 724 (Fla. 1982). What is the rule in jurisdictions that have adopted the Model Penal Code provision on this point? Consider the case that follows.

STATE v. SHAW
_____

Supreme Court of Connecticut
441 A.2d 561 (1981)

SPEZIALE, A.J.

After a trial to a jury the defendant, James Shaw, Jr., was convicted of first degree assault. . . .

The information against the defendant arose from the following incident: Shaw rented one of two bedrooms in a house owned and occupied by Wilson, the person he assaulted. . . . Wilson called Shaw to the common area of the house; a discussion escalated to an argument and then a physical altercation; Wilson and Shaw each claimed that the other initiated the tussle. Wilson went to his bedroom and grabbed his .30-30 Winchester rifle with the intention, as he testified, to order Shaw to leave; Shaw went to his bedroom and got his .22 revolver. Weapons in hand, they both entered the kitchen from their respective bedrooms. The defendant, Shaw, fired five or six shots hitting Wilson three times. . . .

The trial court . . . instructed the jury on self-defense as follows: . . .

> [O]ne section of our statutes reads as follows: "A person is justified in using reasonable physical force upon another person to defend himself . . . except that deadly physical force may not be used unless the actor reasonably believes that such other person is using or about to use, deadly physical force, or inflicting, or about to inflict, great bodily harm."
>
> Now, regardless of those provisions that I just read to you, a person is not justified . . . in using deadly physical force upon another person if he knows that he can avoid the necessity of using such force with complete safety by retreating, except that the actor shall not be required to retreat if he is in his dwelling.
>
> Now, at this point, I would call your attention to the testimony that would indicate that, according to another statutory definition, both Mr. Wilson and Mr. Shaw were in their dwelling. Now, I just don't think that that statute was meant to give them the right, both of them, to refuse to retreat. It would seem to me, where both parties are in their dwelling, retreat must be considered in connection with the question of self-defense. How much force is necessary? Retreat can be taken in a physical way. It can also be taken to mean desist. Here it, apparently, means physically removing yourself from the premises, but it involved also, in this use of force, the idea of desisting when the degree of force you have been using, is no longer necessary. . . .

General Statutes §53a-19 governs the degree of force which a person is justified in using to defend his person. . . . "[A] person is not justified in using deadly physical force upon another person if he knows that he can avoid the necessity of using such force with complete safety (1) by retreating, except that the actor shall not be required to retreat if he is in his dwelling . . . and was not the initial aggressor. . . ." . . . There was conflicting testimony as to who was the "initial aggressor." . . . From the evidence presented the jury reasonably could have found that Shaw had the right to share the use of the kitchen and thus was in "his dwelling" when the shots were fired. . . .

The question before us is whether General Statutes §53a-19 imposes a duty to retreat upon a person in his dwelling when threatened by another person who also dwells in the same place. . . . The statutes which enumerate the situations where the use of force is justified "attempt to restate the common law. They should be read in the light of their common law background, and the fact that an individual section does not fully state the relevant common law rule, with all its possible applications, exceptions or implications, should not prevent a court from reading it as incorporating the full body of common law rules relevant thereto." Commission to Revise the Criminal Statutes, Connecticut Penal Code Comments 5-6 (1972). . . .

When faced with the problem of violence between two persons entitled to occupancy of the same dwelling, American jurisdictions have gone both ways on the issue of a duty to retreat. The majority of jurisdictions have adopted the rule that there is no difference created by the status of the assailant: there is no duty to retreat in one's dwelling whether one's assailant be an intruder or a codweller. . . .

"The rationale behind the no-retreat jurisdictions . . . was inherited from those periods when retreat from one's dwelling was necessarily attended with increased peril. In a civilized country a person's leaving his dwelling does not automatically ordain that he is forsaking a place of safety for one wrought with danger." Note, "Criminal Law — A Further Erosion of the Retreat Rule in North Carolina," 12 Wake Forest L. Rev. 1093, 1100 (1976). . . .

In recognition of the demise of the solitary fortress and the great value of human life the drafters of the Restatement (Second) of Torts have adopted the minority view. "The privilege [to defend oneself against another by force intended or likely to cause death or serious bodily harm] exists although the actor correctly or reasonably believes that he can safely avoid the necessity of so defending himself by (a) retreating if he is attacked within his *dwelling place, which is not also the dwelling place of the other.* . . . The privilege . . . does not exist . . . *in a place which is also the dwelling of the other.* . . ." (Emphasis added.) Restatement (Second), Torts §65 (1965).

We adopt the codweller retreat rule set forth by the Restatement. A minority of jurisdictions have long recognized it. This rule is in line with a policy favoring human life over the burden of retreating from the home, and the usual self-defense principles would still apply to allow defense at the wall or where retreat is impossible. In the great majority of homicides the killer and the victim are relatives or close acquaintances. We cannot conclude that the Connecticut legislature intended to sanction the reenactment of the climactic scene from "High Noon" in the familial kitchens of this state. The trial court did not err in not giving the defendant's requested instruction that he had no duty to retreat from his codweller even if he could safely do so. . . .

BOGDANSKI, C.J. (dissenting).

I do not dispute the wisdom of the exception that the court adds to the statutory "no retreat" rule. I note, however, that

> as far back as 1821 this court held that penal statutes must be . . . "expounded strictly against an offender, and liberally in his favor. . . . In extension of the letter of the law, nothing may be assumed by implication; nor may the mischief *intended* to be prevented or redressed, as against the offender, be regarded in its construction. It was the object of the principle, to establish a certain rule, by conformity to which mankind should be safe, and the discretion of the judge limited. . . ." Daggett v. State, 4 Conn. 60, 63 [1821].

General Statutes §53a-19(b)(1) recognizes only one exception to the rule that a person, in his dwelling, need not retreat before resorting to a deadly physical defense in a reasonable belief that another person is (1) using or about to use deadly physical force, or (2) inflicting or about to inflict great bodily harm. That exception denies the benefit of the rule to an initial aggressor. Today the court adds a second exception to the rule and thereby makes criminal the failure to retreat in one's dwelling before resorting to deadly physical force in self-defense against . . . an initial aggressor who happens to be a co-occupant of the dwelling. Such an act is not encompassed by the plain meaning of the penal code. . . . [A]doption of the new exception abandons the rule of strict construction and violates the constitutional guarantee of due process by making the defendant's conduct criminal without having given him a reasonable opportunity to know that it was prohibited and to act accordingly.

Furthermore, General Statutes §53a-19(b)(1) is based on comparable provisions of the New York Penal Code and the Model Penal Code. The commentary to the comparable section of the Model Penal Code states: "The Institute voted not to require retreat from the actor's dwelling when he is assailed by another person whose dwelling it also is. . . ." In view of the plain language and the derivation of §53a-19(b)(1), I believe that the majority usurps the legislature's authority by rejecting the statute's limitation on the retreat doctrine. . . .

Page 757. Replace Mattis v. Schnarr with the following:

TENNESSEE v. GARNER

Supreme Court of the United States
105 S. Ct. 1964 (1985)

WHITE, J., delivered the opinion of the Court.

This case requires us to determine the constitutionality of the use of deadly force to prevent the escape of an apparently unarmed suspected felon. We conclude that such force may not be used unless it is necessary to prevent the escape and the officer has probable cause to believe that the suspect poses a significant threat of death or serious physical injury to the officer or others.

At about 10:45 P.M. on October 3, 1974, Memphis Police Officers Elton Hymon and Leslie Wright were dispatched to answer a "prowler inside call." Upon arriving at the scene they saw a woman standing on her porch and gesturing toward the adjacent house. She told them she had heard glass breaking and that "they" or "someone" was breaking in next door. While Wright radioed the dispatcher to say that they were on the scene, Hymon went behind the house. He heard a door slam and saw someone run across the back yard. The fleeing suspect, who was appellee-respondent's decedent, Edward Garner, stopped at a 6-feet-high chain link fence at the edge of the yard. With the aid of a flashlight, Hymon was able to see Garner's face and hands. He saw no sign of a weapon, and, though not certain, was "reasonably sure" and "figured" that Garner was unarmed. He thought Garner was 17 or 18 years old and about 5'5" or 5'7" tall.[2] While Garner was crouched at the base of the fence, Hymon called out "police, halt" and took a few steps toward him. Garner then began to climb over the fence. Convinced that if Garner made it over the fence he would elude capture,[3] Hymon

---

2. In fact, Garner, an eighth-grader, was 15. He was 5'4" tall and weighed somewhere around 100 or 110 pounds.

3. When asked at trial why he fired, Hymon stated:

"Well, first of all it was apparent to me from the little bit that I knew about the area at the time that he was going to get away because, number 1, I couldn't get to him. My partner then couldn't find where he was because, you know, he was late coming around. He didn't know where I was talking about. I couldn't get to him because of the fence here, I couldn't have jumped this fence and come up, consequently jumped this fence and caught him before he got away because he was already up on the fence, just one leap and he was already over the fence, and so there is no way that I could have caught him."

He also stated that the area beyond the fence was dark, that he could not have gotten over the fence easily because he was carrying a lot of equipment and wearing heavy boots, and that Garner, being younger and more energetic, could have outrun him.

shot him. The bullet hit Garner in the back of the head. Garner was taken by ambulance to a hospital, where he died on the operating table. Ten dollars and a purse taken from the house were found on his body.

In using deadly force to prevent the escape, Hymon was acting under the authority of a Tennessee statute and pursuant to Police Department policy. The statute provides that "[i]f, after notice of the intention to arrest the defendant, he either flee or forcibly resist, the officer may use all the necessary means to effect the arrest." Tenn. Code Ann. §40-7-108 (1982).[5] The Department policy was slightly more restrictive than the statute, but still allowed the use of deadly force in cases of burglary. The incident was reviewed by the Memphis Police Firearm's Review Board and presented to a grand jury. Neither took any action.

Garner's father then brought this action in the Federal District Court for the Western District of Tennessee, seeking damages under 42 U.S.C. §1983 for asserted violations of Garner's constitutional rights. The complaint alleged that the shooting violated the Fourth, Fifth, Sixth, Eighth, and Fourteenth Amendments of the United States Constitution. It named as defendants Officer Hymon, the Police Department, its Director, and the Mayor and city of Memphis. . . . [T]he District Court entered judgment for all defendants. . . . It . . . concluded that Hymon's actions were authorized by the Tennessee statute, which in turn was constitutional. Hymon had employed the only reasonable and practicable means of preventing Garner's escape. Garner had "recklessly and heedlessly attempted to vault over the fence to escape, thereby assuming the risk of being fired upon." . . .

The Court of Appeals reversed and remanded. It reasoned that the killing of a fleeing suspect is a "seizure" under the Fourth Amendment,[6] and is therefore constitutional only if "reasonable." . . .[7]

The State of Tennessee, which had intervened to defend the statute, appealed to this Court. . . .

Whenever an officer restrains the freedom of a person to walk away, he has seized that person. While it is not always clear just when minimal police interference becomes a seizure, there can be no question that apprehension by the use of deadly force is a seizure subject to the reasonableness requirement of the Fourth Amendment.

5. Although the statute does not say so explicitly, Tennessee law forbids the use of deadly force in the arrest of a misdemeanant.

6. "The right of the people to be secure in their persons . . . against unreasonable searches and seizures, shall not be violated. . . ." U.S. Const., Amdt. 4.

7. The Court of Appeals concluded that the rule set out in the Model Penal Code "accurately states Fourth Amendment limitations on the use of deadly force against fleeing felons." . . .

A police officer may arrest a person if he has probable cause to believe that person committed a crime. E.g., United States v. Watson, 423 U.S. 411 (1976). Petitioners and appellant argue that if this requirement is satisfied the Fourth Amendment has nothing to say about *how* that seizure is made. This submission ignores the many cases in which this Court, by balancing the extent of the intrusion against the need for it, has examined the reasonableness of the manner in which a search or seizure is conducted. . . .

Applying these principles to particular facts, the Court has held that governmental interests did not support a lengthy detention of luggage, United States v. Place, [462 U.S. 696 (1983)], . . . surgery under general anesthesia to obtain evidence, Winston v. Lee, — U.S. — (1985), or detention for fingerprinting without probable cause, Davis v. Mississippi, 394 U.S. 721 (1969); Hayes v. Florida, — U.S. — (1985). On the other hand, under the same approach it has upheld the taking of fingernail scrapings from a suspect, Cupp v. Murphy, 412 U.S. 291 (1973), . . . and a blood test of a drunk-driving suspect, Schmerber v. California, 384 U.S. 757 (1966). In each of these cases, the question was whether the totality of the circumstances justified a particular sort of search or seizure.

The same balancing process applied in the cases cited above demonstrates that, notwithstanding probable cause to seize a suspect, an officer may not always do so by killing him. The intrusiveness of a seizure by means of deadly force is unmatched. The suspect's fundamental interest in his own life need not be elaborated upon. The use of deadly force also frustrates the interest of the individual, and of society, in judicial determination of guilt and punishment. Against these interests are ranged governmental interests in effective law enforcement.[8] It is argued that overall violence will be reduced by encouraging the peaceful submission of suspects who know that they may be shot if they flee. . . . "Being able to arrest such individuals is a condition precedent to the state's entire system of law enforcement."

Without in any way disparaging the importance of these goals, we are not convinced that the use of deadly force is a sufficiently productive means of accomplishing them to justify the killing of nonviolent suspects. The use of deadly force is a self-defeating way of apprehending a suspect and so setting the criminal justice mechanism in motion. If

8. The dissent emphasizes that subsequent investigation cannot replace immediate apprehension. We recognize that this is so; indeed, that is the reason why there is any dispute. If subsequent arrest were assured, no one would argue that use of deadly force was justified. Thus, we proceed on the assumption that subsequent arrest is not likely. Nonetheless, it should be remembered that failure to apprehend at the scene does not necessarily mean that the suspect will never be caught. . . .

successful, it guarantees that that mechanism will not be set in motion. And while the meaningful threat of deadly force might be thought to lead to the arrest of more live suspects by discouraging escape attempts,[9] the presently available evidence does not support this thesis. The fact is that a majority of police departments in this country have forbidden the use of deadly force against nonviolent suspects. If those charged with the enforcement of the criminal law have abjured the use of deadly force in arresting nondangerous felons, there is a substantial basis for doubting that the use of such force is an essential attribute of the arrest power in all felony cases. Petitioners and appellant have not persuaded us that shooting nondangerous fleeing suspects is so vital as to outweigh the suspect's interest in his own life.

The use of deadly force to prevent the escape of all felony suspects, whatever the circumstances, is constitutionally unreasonable. It is not better that all felony suspects die than that they escape. It is no doubt unfortunate when a suspect who is in sight escapes, but the fact that the police arrive a little late or are a little slower afoot does not always justify killing the suspect. A police officer may not seize an unarmed, nondangerous suspect by shooting him dead. The Tennessee statute is unconstitutional insofar as it authorizes the use of deadly force against such fleeing suspects.

It is not, however, unconstitutional on its face. Where the officer has probable cause to believe that the suspect poses a threat of serious physical harm, either to the officer or to others, it is not constitutionally unreasonable to prevent escape by using deadly force. Thus, if the suspect threatens the officer with a weapon or there is probable cause to believe that he has committed a crime involving the infliction or threatened infliction of serious physical harm, deadly force may be used if necessary to prevent escape, and if, where feasible, some warning has been given. As applied in such circumstances, the Tennessee statute would pass constitutional muster.

It is insisted that the Fourth Amendment must be construed in light of the common-law rule, which allowed the use of whatever force was necessary to effect the arrest of a fleeing felon, though not a misdemeanant. . . .

---

9. We note that the usual manner of deterring illegal conduct—through punishment—has been largely ignored in connection with flight from arrest. Arkansas, for example, specifically excepts flight from arrest from the offense of "obstruction of governmental operations." The commentary notes that this "reflects the basic policy judgment that, absent the use of force or violence, a mere attempt to avoid apprehension by a law enforcement officer does not give rise to an independent offense." Ark. Stat. Ann. §41-2802(3)(a) (1977) and commentary. In the few States that do outlaw flight from an arresting officer, the crime is only a misdemeanor. . . .

The State and city argue that because this was the prevailing rule at the time of the adoption of the Fourth Amendment and for some time thereafter, and is still in force in some States, use of deadly force against a fleeing felon must be "reasonable." It is true that this Court has often looked to the common law in evaluating the reasonableness, for Fourth Amendment purposes, of police activity. On the other hand, it "has not simply frozen into constitutional law those law enforcement practices that existed at the time of the Fourth Amendment's passage." Because of sweeping change in the legal and technological context, reliance on the common-law rule in this case would be a mistaken literalism that ignores the purposes of a historical inquiry.

It has been pointed out many times that the common-law rule is best understood in light of the fact that it arose at a time when virtually all felonies were punishable by death. "Though effected without the protections and formalities of an orderly trial and conviction, the killing of a resisting or fleeing felon resulted in no greater consequences than those authorized for punishment of the felony of which the individual was charged or suspected." American Law Institute, Model Penal Code §3.07, Comment 3, p.56 (Tentative Draft No. 8, 1958). Courts have also justified the common-law rule by emphasizing the relative dangerousness of felons.

Neither of these justifications makes sense today. Almost all crimes formerly punishable by death no longer are or can be. See, e.g., Enmund v. Florida, 458 U.S. 782 (1982); Coker v. Georgia, 433 U.S. 584 (1977). And while in earlier times "the gulf between the felonies and the minor offences was broad and deep," 2 Pollock & Maitland 467, n.3, today the distinction is minor and often arbitrary. Many crimes classified as misdemeanors . . . at common law are now felonies. These changes have undermined the concept, which was questionable to begin with, that use of deadly force against a fleeing felon is merely a speedier execution of someone who has already forfeited his life. They have also made the assumption that a "felon" is more dangerous than a misdemeanant untenable. Indeed, numerous misdemeanors involve conduct more dangerous than many felonies.[12]

There is an additional reason why the common-law rule cannot be directly translated to the present day. The common-law rule developed at a time when weapons were rudimentary. Deadly force could be inflicted almost solely in a hand-to-hand struggle during which, necessarily, the safety of the arresting officer was at risk. Handguns were not carried by police officers until the latter half of the last century.

---

12. White collar crime, for example, poses a less significant physical threat than, say, drunken driving.

L. Kennett & J. Anderson, The Gun in America 150-151 (1975). Only
then did it become possible to use deadly force from a distance as a
means of apprehension. As a practical matter, the use of deadly force
under the standard articulation of the common-law rule has an altogether different meaning—and harsher consequences—now than in
past centuries. See Wechsler & Michael, A Rationale for the Law of
Homicide: I, 37 Colum. L. Rev. 701, 741 (1937). . . .

In short, . . . changes in the legal and technological context mean the
rule is distorted almost beyond recognition when literally applied.

In evaluating the reasonableness of police procedures under the
Fourth Amendment, we have also looked to prevailing rules in individual jurisdictions. Some 19 States have codified the common-law
rule. . . . Four States, though without a relevant statute, apparently retain the common-law rule. Two States have adopted the Model Penal
Code's provision verbatim. Eighteen others allow, in slightly varying
language, the use of deadly force only if the suspect has committed a
felony involving the use or threat of physical or deadly force, or is
escaping with a deadly weapon, or is likely to endanger life or inflict
serious physical injury if not arrested. . . .

It cannot be said that there is a constant or overwhelming trend away
from the common-law rule. . . . Nonetheless, the long-term movement
has been away from the rule that deadly force may be used against any
fleeing felon, and that remains the rule in less than half the States.

This trend is more evident and impressive when viewed in light of
the policies adopted by the police departments themselves. Overwhelm-
ingly, these are more restrictive than the common-law rule. C. Milton,
J. Halleck, J. Lardner, & G. Abrecht, Police Use of Deadly Force 45-46
(1977). The Federal Bureau of Investigation and the New York City
Police Department, for example, both forbid the use of firearms except
when necessary to prevent death or grievous bodily harm. . . . Overall,
only 7.5% of departmental and municipal policies explicitly permit the
use of deadly force against any felon; 86.8% explicitly do not. In light
of the rules adopted by those who must actually administer them, the
older and fading common-law view is a dubious indicium of the constitutionality of the Tennessee statute now before us.

Actual departmental policies are important for an additional reason.
We would hesitate to declare a police practice of long standing "unreasonable" if doing so would severely hamper effective law enforcement.
But the indications are to the contrary. . . . Amici note that "[a]fter
extensive research and consideration, [they] have concluded that laws
permitting police officers to use deadly force to apprehend unarmed,
non-violent fleeing felony suspects actually do not protect citizens or
law enforcement officers, do not deter crime or alleviate problems

caused by crime, and do not improve the crime-fighting ability of law enforcement agencies." Brief for Police Foundation et al. as Amici Curiae 11. . . .

In reversing, the Court of Appeals accepted the District Court's factual conclusions and held that "the facts, as found, did not justify the use of deadly force." We agree. Officer Hymon could not reasonably have believed that Garner—young, slight, and unarmed—posed any threat. Indeed, Hymon never attempted to justify his actions on any basis other than the need to prevent an escape. . . .

The dissent argues that the shooting was justified by the fact that Officer Hymon had probable cause to believe that Garner had committed a nighttime burglary. While we agree that burglary is a serious crime, we cannot agree that it is so dangerous as automatically to justify the use of deadly force. . . . Although the armed burglar would present a different situation, the fact that an unarmed suspect has broken into a dwelling at night does not automatically mean he is physically dangerous. This case demonstrates as much. In fact, the available statistics demonstrate that burglaries only rarely involve physical violence. During the 10-year period from 1973-1982, only 3.8% of all burglaries involved violent crime. Bureau of Justice Statistics, Household Burglary, p.4 (1985).[23] . . .

The judgment of the Court of Appeals is affirmed. . . .

So ordered.

O'CONNOR, J., with whom THE CHIEF JUSTICE and REHNQUIST, J., join, dissenting.

. . . [I]t is crucial to acknowledge that police use of deadly force to apprehend a fleeing criminal suspect falls within the "rubric of police conduct . . . necessarily [involving] swift action predicated upon the on-the-spot observations of the officer on the beat." Terry v. Ohio, 392 U.S. 1, 20 (1968). The clarity of hindsight cannot provide the standard for judging the reasonableness of police decisions made in uncertain and often dangerous circumstances. Moreover, I am far more reluctant than

23. The dissent points out that three-fifths of all rapes in the home, three-fifths of all home robberies, and about a third of home assaults are committed by burglars. These figures mean only that if one knows that a suspect committed a rape in the home, there is a good chance that the suspect is also a burglar. That has nothing to do with the question here, which is whether the fact that someone has committed a burglary indicates that he has committed, or might commit, a violent crime.

The dissent also points out that this 3.8% adds up to 2.8 million violent crimes over a 10-year period, as if to imply that today's holding will let loose 2.8 million violent burglars. The relevant universe is, of course, far smaller. At issue is only that tiny fraction of cases where violence has taken place and an officer who has no other means of apprehending the suspect is unaware of its occurrence.

is the Court to conclude that the Fourth Amendment proscribes a police practice that was accepted at the time of the adoption of the Bill of Rights and has continued to receive the support of many state legislatures. Although the Court has recognized that the requirements of the Fourth Amendment must respond to the reality of social and technological change, fidelity to the notion of *constitutional* — as opposed to purely judicial — limits on governmental action requires us to impose a heavy burden on those who claim that practices accepted when the Fourth Amendment was adopted are now constitutionally impermissible.

The public interest involved in the use of deadly force as a last resort to apprehend a fleeing burglary suspect relates primarily to the serious nature of the crime. Household burglaries represent not only the illegal entry into a person's home, but also "pos[e] real risk of serious harm to others." Solem v. Helm, 463 U.S. 277, 315-316 (1983) (Burger, C.J., dissenting). According to recent Department of Justice statistics, "[t]hree-fifths of all rapes in the home, three-fifths of all home robberies, and about a third of home aggravated and simple assaults are committed by burglars." During the period 1973-1982, 2.8 million such violent crimes were committed in the course of burglaries. Victims of a forcible intrusion into their home by a nighttime prowler will find little consolation in the majority's confident assertion that "burglaries only rarely involve physical violence." Moreover, even if a particular burglary, when viewed in retrospect, does not involve physical harm to others, the "harsh potentialities for violence" inherent in the forced entry into a home preclude characterization of the crime as "innocuous, inconsequential, minor, or 'nonviolent.' " Solem v. Helm, supra, at 316 (Burger, C.J., dissenting).

Because burglary is a serious and dangerous felony, the public interest in the prevention and detection of the crime is of compelling importance. Where a police officer has probable cause to arrest a suspected burglar, the use of deadly force as a last resort might well be the only means of apprehending the suspect. With respect to a particular burglary, subsequent investigation simply cannot represent a substitute for immediate apprehension of the criminal suspect at the scene. Indeed, the Captain of the Memphis Police Department testified that in his city, if apprehension is not immediate, it is likely that the suspect will not be caught. Although some law enforcement agencies may choose to assume the risk that a criminal will remain at large, the Tennessee statute reflects a legislative determination that the use of deadly force in prescribed circumstances will serve generally to protect the public. . . .

The Court unconvincingly dismisses the general deterrence effects by stating that "the presently available evidence does not support [the] thesis" that the threat of force discourages escape and that "there is a substantial basis for doubting that the use of such force is an essential attribute to the arrest power in all felony cases." . . . But it should go without saying that the effectiveness or popularity of a particular police practice does not determine its constitutionality. Moreover, the fact that police conduct pursuant to a state statute is challenged on constitutional grounds does not impose a burden on the State to produce social statistics or to dispel any possible doubts about the necessity of the conduct. . . .

. . . The majority declares that "[t]he suspect's fundamental interest in his own life need not be elaborated upon." This blithe assertion hardly provides an adequate substitute for the majority's failure to acknowledge the distinctive manner in which the suspect's interest in his life is even exposed to risk. . . . The officer's use of force resulted because the suspected burglar refused to heed [his] command [to halt] and the officer reasonably believed that there was no means short of firing his weapon to apprehend the suspect. Without questioning the importance of a person's interest in his life, I do not think this interest encompasses a right to flee unimpeded from the scene of a burglary. . . . The legitimate interests of the suspect in these circumstances are adequately accommodated by the Tennessee statute: to avoid the use of deadly force and the consequent risk to his life, the suspect need merely obey the valid order to halt. . . .

The Court's silence on critical factors in the decision to use deadly force invites second-guessing of difficult police . . . decisions that must be made quickly in the most trying of circumstances. Police are given no guidance for determining which objects, among an array of potentially lethal weapons ranging from guns to knives to baseball bats to rope, will justify the use of deadly force. The Court also declines to outline the additional factors necessary to provide "probable cause" for believing that a suspect "poses a significant threat of death or serious physical injury." . . . We can expect an escalating volume of litigation as the lower courts struggle to determine if a police officer's split-second decision to shoot was justified by the danger posed by a particular object and other facts related to the crime.

. . . Whatever the constitutional limits on police use of deadly force in order to apprehend a fleeing felon, I do not believe they are exceeded in a case in which a police officer has probable cause to arrest a suspect at the scene of a residential burglary, orders the suspect to halt, and then fires his weapon as a last resort to prevent the suspect's escape into the night. I respectfully dissent.

Page 781. Before Problem 2 insert:

Anti-abortion protesters continue in their efforts to defend against trespass charges by invoking the defense of necessity. In Cleveland v.

Municipality of Anchorage, 632 P.2d 1073 (Alaska 1981), the Alaska Supreme Court held the defense unavailable on the grounds that the "necessity" generally must result from the "physical forces of nature"; that defendants had alternative, lawful means of protest available; and that the harm sought to be averted (the killing of innocent fetuses) was not greater than the harm that foreseeably resulted from the protest (disruption of the abortion clinic's activities and interference with the right of privacy of its patients).

Page 797. Before Problem 2 add:

1a. In Regina v. Graham, noted in [1982] Crim. L. Rev. 465, the defendant, a homosexual who had been drinking and taking drugs, claimed that his homosexual partner threatened to kill him if he did not help the partner kill the defendant's wife; the two then strangled the wife with an electric cord. Apparently, the plug that the defendant was holding came off, and there was therefore some doubt about whether the defendant's own acts contributed to his wife's death. Query: Can the defendant invoke the defense of duress? Recall that under the English decisions (which probably would be followed in many American jurisdictions) the actual killer cannot raise the duress defense to a murder charge, Abbott v. The Queen, [1976] 3 All E.R. 140, but one charged as an accomplice can do so, Lynch v. Director of Public Prosecutions, Casebook page 797. The distinction between principal and accomplice can therefore have major consequences; Abbott — who had a substantial claim of duress — was hanged for his crime. In *Graham* the court said: "[T]he jury would no doubt be puzzled to learn that whether the appellant was to be convicted of murder or acquitted altogether might depend on whether the plug came off the end of the [electric cord] when he began to pull it." [1982] Crim. L. Rev., at 367. Commenting on this case, Professor J. C. Smith concluded that "no valid distinction can be made between the principal in the first degree and secondary parties in murder." Id.

If principals and accomplices should receive the same treatment, should the defense of duress be available to both or to neither? In favor of granting the defense, even to murder, it is argued that the law should not exact a degree of heroism of which the ordinary person is, by definition, incapable. On the other hand, consider the comments of Lord Salmon, arguing in *Abbott,* supra, that the defense should be denied ([1976] 3 All E.R. at 146):

> In the trials of those responsible for wartime atrocities such as mass killings of men, women or children, inhuman experiments on human beings, often

resulting in death, and like crimes, it was invariably argued for the defence that these atrocities should be excused on the ground that they resulted from superior orders and duress: if the accused had refused to do these dreadful things, they would have been shot and therefore they should be acquitted and allowed to go free. This argument has always been universally rejected. Their Lordships would be sorry indeed to see it accepted by the common law of England.

. . . A terrorist of notorious violence might, e.g., threaten death to A and his family unless A obeys his instructions to put a bomb with a time fuse set by A in a certain passenger aircraft and/or in a thronged market, railway station or the like. . . . Is there any limit to the number of people you may kill to save your own life and that of your family?

Page 815. After line 4 insert the following new Note:

2a. An Indiana statute provides that "[v]oluntary intoxication is a defense only to the extent that it negatives an element of an offense referred to by the phrase 'with intent' or 'with intention to.' " In an attempted murder case, the prosecution argued that voluntary intoxication was not a defense with respect to this offense, traditionally one of specific intent, because the attempt statute did not contain the precise phrase "with intent" or "with an intention to." In Terry v. State, 465 N.E.2d 1085 (Ind. 1984), the Indiana Supreme Court declined to construe the statutory phrases as extending to crimes interpreted to require a specific intent. Rather, that court held evidence of voluntary intoxication admissible without regard to the nature of the offense charged and ruled the Indiana statute unconstitutional. The court said (id. at 1088):

> Any factor which serves as a denial of the existence of mens rea must be considered by a trier of fact before a guilty finding is entered. Historically, facts such as age, mental condition, mistake or intoxication have been offered to negate the capacity to formulate intent. The attempt by the legislature to remove the factor of voluntary intoxication, except in limited situations, goes against this firmly ingrained principle. We thus hold Ind. Code §35-41-3-5(b) is void and without effect.

Page 831. Before United States v. Brawner insert:

NOTE

An initiative measure passed in 1982 overturned *Drew* and reestablished the *M'Naghten* test in California. See this Supplement pages 88-89 infra.

Page 839. After the carryover paragraph insert:

UNITED STATES v. LYONS

United States Court of Appeals, Fifth Circuit, en banc
731 F.2d 243, 739 F.2d 994 (1984)

GEE, C.J.
Defendant Robert Lyons was indicted on twelve counts of knowingly and intentionally securing controlled narcotics. . . . Lyons proffered evidence that in 1978 he began to suffer from several painful ailments, that various narcotics were prescribed to be taken as needed for his pain, and that he became addicted to these drugs. He also offered to present expert witnesses who would testify that his drug addiction affected his brain both physiologically and psychologically and that as a result he lacked substantial capacity to conform his conduct to the requirements of the law. . . .

[The trial court excluded the proffered evidence, and Lyons was convicted.]

Today the great weight of legal authority clearly supports the view that evidence of mere narcotics addiction, standing alone and without other physiological or psychological involvement, raises no issue of such a mental defect or disease as can serve as a basis for the insanity defense. . . .[a]

We do not doubt that actual physical damage to the brain itself falls within the ambit of "mental disease or defect." . . .

Lyons asserted by his proffer of evidence that his drug addiction caused physiological damage to his brain and that this damage caused him to lack substantial capacity to conform his conduct to the requirements of the law. . . . Because the proffer offers evidence tending to suggest such damage, that evidence should have been submitted to the jury. And although we today withdraw our recognition of the volitional prong of [the insanity defense]—that as to which such evidence has usually been advanced—we also conclude that should Lyons wish to offer such evidence in an attempt to satisfy the remaining cognitive prong, fairness demands that we afford him an opportunity to do so.

. . . We last examined the insanity defense in Blake v. United States, 407 F.2d 908 (5th Cir. 1969) (en banc), where we adopted the ALI Model Penal Code definition of insanity: that a person is not responsible for criminal conduct if, at the time of such conduct and as a result of mental disease or defect, he lacks substantial capacity either to appreciate the wrongfulness of his conduct or to conform his conduct to the requirements of the law. . . . [W]e concluded that then current

a. See Casebook pages 893-901.

knowledge in the field of behavioral science supported such a result. Unfortunately, it now appears our conclusion was premature. . . .

Reexamining the *Blake* standard today, we conclude that the volitional prong of the insanity defense—a lack of capacity to conform one's conduct to the requirements of the law—does not comport with current medical and scientific knowledge, which has retreated from its earlier, sanguine expectations. Consequently, we now hold that a person is not responsible for criminal conduct on the grounds of insanity only if at the time of that conduct, as a result of a mental disease or defect, he is unable to appreciate the wrongfulness of that conduct.[9]

We do so for several reasons. First, as we have mentioned, a majority of psychiatrists now believe that they do not possess sufficient accurate scientific bases for measuring a person's capacity for self-control or for calibrating the impairment of that capacity. Bonnie, The Moral Basis of the Insanity Defense, 69 A.B.A.J. 194, 196 (1983). "The line between an irresistible impulse and an impulse not resisted is probably no sharper than between twilight and dusk." American Psychiatric Association Statement on the Insanity Defense, 11 (1982) [APA Statement]. Indeed, Professor Bonnie states:

> There is, in short, no objective basis for distinguishing between offenders who were undeterrable and those who were merely undeterred, between the impulse that was irresistible and the impulse not resisted, or between substantial impairment of capacity and some lesser impairment.

Bonnie, supra, at 196.[11]

---

9. We employ the phrase "is unable" in preference to our earlier formulation "lacks substantial capacity" for reasons well stated in the Commentary of the American Bar Association Standing Committee:

> . . . [T]he standard employs the term "unable" in lieu of the "substantial capacity" language of the ALI test. This approach has been taken both to simplify the formulation and to reduce the risk that juries will interpret the test too loosely. By using the "substantial capacity" language, the drafters of the ALI standard were trying to avoid the rigidity implicit in the M'Naughten formulation. They correctly recognize that it is rarely possible to say that a mentally disordered person was totally unable to "know" what he was doing or to "know" that it was wrong; even a psychotic person typically retains some grasp of reality. However, the phrase "substantial capacity" is not essential to take into account these clinical realities. Sufficient flexibility is provided by the term "appreciate."

Commentary (revised November, 1983) to Standards 7-6.1(a) and 7-6.9(b), ABA Standing Committee on Association Standards for Criminal Justice (to be published).

11. One commentator has noted that no one has ever observed the process of a person losing the capacity for self-control, and "that no one can." [H. Fingarette, The Meaning of Insanity 160 (1972).]

In addition, the risks of fabrication and "moral mistakes" in administering the insanity defense are greatest "when the experts and the jury are asked to speculate whether the defendant had the capacity to 'control' himself or whether he could have 'resisted' the criminal impulse." Bonnie, supra, at 196. Moreover, psychiatric testimony about volition is more likely to produce confusion for jurors than is psychiatric testimony concerning a defendant's appreciation of the wrongfulness of his act. It appears, moreover, that there is considerable overlap between a psychotic person's inability to understand and his ability to control his behavior. Most psychotic persons who fail a volitional test would also fail a cognitive test, thus rendering the volitional test superfluous for them. Finally, Supreme Court authority requires that such proof be made by the federal prosecutor beyond a reasonable doubt, an all but impossible task in view of the present murky state of medical knowledge. Davis v. United States, 160 U.S. 469 (1895).[13]

. . . [W]e see no prudent course for the law to follow but to treat all criminal impulses — including those not resisted — as resistible. To do otherwise in the present state of medical knowledge would be to cast the insanity defense adrift upon a sea of unfounded scientific speculation, with the palm awarded case by case to the most convincing advocate of that which is presently unknown — and may remain so, because unknowable. . . .

RUBIN, J., with whom TATE, J., joins dissenting. . . .

. . . An adjudication of guilt is more than a factual determination that the defendant pulled a trigger, took a bicycle, or sold heroin. It is a moral judgment that the individual is blameworthy. "Our collective conscience does not allow punishment where it cannot impose blame." . . . "[H]istorically, our substantive criminal law is based on a theory of punishing the [vicious] will. It postulates a free agent confronted with a choice between doing right and wrong, and choosing freely to do wrong."[3] . . . An acquittal by reason of insanity is a judgment that the

13. [Johnson, Book Review, 50 U. Chi. L. Rev. 1534. 1536 (1983) (reviewing N. Morris, Madness and the Criminal Law (1982)):]

    . . . If taken literally, the instruction [requiring proof of sanity beyond a reasonable doubt in the John Hinckley prosecution] amounted to a directed verdict of not guilty, considering the deadlock of expert opinion and the difficulty of certifying the sanity of a young man who shot the President to impress a movie star. Juries usually ignore such unpopular legal standards, but the *Hinckley* jury surprised everybody by taking the law seriously and finding him not guilty. Hinckley will now be confined to a mental hospital indefinitely because he is "dangerous," although there is no reliable way to predict what he would do if released and no reliable test to determine if he has been "cured."

3. Morissette v. United States, 342 U.S. 246, 250 n.4 (1952) (quoting Pound, Introduction to Sayre, Cases on Criminal Law (1927)).

defendant is not *guilty* because, as a result of his mental condition, he is unable to make an effective choice regarding his behavior.

The majority does not controvert these fundamental principles; indeed it accepts them as the basis for the defense when the accused suffers from a disease that impairs cognition. It rests its decision to redefine insanity and to narrow the defense on "new policy considerations." . . .

The first is the potential threat to society created by the volitional prong of the insanity defense. Public opposition to any insanity-grounded defense is often based, either explicitly or implicitly, on the view that the plea is frequently invoked by violent criminals who fraudulently use it to evade just punishment. . . . This perception depicts an insanity trial as a "circus" of conflicting expert testimony that confuses a naive and sympathetic jury. And it fears insanity acquittees as offenders who, after manipulating the criminal justice system, are soon set free to prey once again on the community.

Despite the prodigious volume of writing devoted to the plea, the empirical data that are available provide little or no support for these fearsome perceptions and in many respects directly refute them. Both the frequency and the success rate of insanity pleas are grossly overestimated by professionals and lay persons alike; the plea is rarely made, and even more rarely successful.[8] The number of insanity pleas based on control defects, as compared to those based on lack of cognition, must have been almost negligible.

The perception that the defendant who successfully pleads insanity is quickly released from custody is also based only on assumption. . . . "The truth is that in almost every case, the acquittee is immediately hospitalized and evaluated for dangerousness. Usually, the acquittee remains hospitalized for an extended time."[9] . . .

Another set of objections to the plea is based on the thesis that factfinders — especially juries — are confused and manipulated by the vagueness of the legal standards of insanity and the notorious "battle of the experts" who present conclusory, superficial, and misleading testimony. These conditions, the argument runs, conspire to produce inconsistent and "inaccurate" verdicts.

---

8. For example, one extensive study examined the opinions held by college students, the general public, state legislators, law enforcement officers, and mental health personnel in Wyoming. Estimates of the frequency with which criminal defendants entered the plea ranged from 13% to 57%. During the time period considered, however, the actual frequency was only 0.47%: one case in 200. Similarly, although estimates of its success rate varied from 19% to 44%, during the relevant period only one of the 102 defendants who entered the plea was acquitted by reason of insanity. . . .

9. Rappeport, The Insanity Plea Scapegoating the Mentally Ill—Much Ado about Nothing?, 24 So. Tex. L.J. 687, 698 (1983). . . .

Let us first put these objections in perspective. Most cases involving an insanity plea do not go to trial; instead, like most other criminal cases, they are settled by a plea bargain. In many of the cases that do go to trial, psychiatric testimony is presented by deposition, without disagreement among experts, and without opposition by the prosecution. And in the few cases in which a contest does develop, the defendant is usually convicted. . . .

The manipulated-jury argument is supported largely by declamation, not data. . . . Although the evidence does not warrant the conclusion that juries function better in insanity trials than in other criminal cases, it certainly does not appear that they function *less* effectively. And no source has been cited to the court to support the conclusion that, as an empirical matter, pleas based upon the volitional prong present an especially problematic task for the jury.

Indeed, the majority opinion does not assert that the insanity defense, particularly the control test, *doesn't* work; it contends that the defense *can't* work. The principal basis for this contention is the belief, held by "a majority of psychiatrists," that they lack "sufficient accurate scientific bases for measuring a person's capacity for self-control or for calibrating the impairment of that capacity." This argument raises practical and important questions regarding the usefulness of expert testimony in determining whether a person has the ability to conform his conduct to law; but the absence of useful expert evidence, if indeed there is none, does not obviate the need for resolving the question whether the defendant ought to be held accountable for his criminal behavior. . . .

Our concept of responsibility in this sense is not limited to observable behavior: it embraces *meaningful* choice, and necessarily requires inferences and assumptions regarding the defendant's unobservable mental state. . . . The difference between the concepts of excusing circumstances such as coercion and the insanity defense is that the former is based on objective assumptions about human behavior and is tested against hypothetical-objective standards such as "the reasonable person." "The insanity defense [on the other hand] marks the transition from the adequate man the law demands to the inadequate man he may be."[17]

The relevant inquiry under either branch of the insanity test is a subjective one that focuses on the defendant's actual state of mind. Our duty to undertake that inquiry is not based on confidence in the testimony of expert witnesses, but on the ethical precept that the defen-

17. A. Goldstein, The Insanity Defense 18 (1967).

dant's mental state is a crucial aspect of his blameworthiness. . . . The availability of expert testimony and the probative value of such testimony are basically evidentiary problems that can be accommodated within the existing test. . . .

Even the few cases in which the trial develops into a battle of experts provide no basis for the majority's conclusion that the prosecution faces an "all but impossible task." The prosecution appears to be able to locate experts as readily as the defense. Indeed, a defendant pleading insanity typically faces both a judge and a jury who are skeptical about psychiatry in general and the insanity plea in particular. Sharply adversarial presentation of conflicting psychiatric testimony may increase this skepticism, and thus make acquittal more unlikely. Usually the defendant will have been adjudicated sane enough to understand the proceedings against him and to assist in his defense: otherwise he would be incompetent to stand trial. The formal allocation of the persuasion burden notwithstanding, the defendant to prevail must convince the doubting factfinder that, despite present outward appearances, he was insane at the time he committed the crime.

The majority's fear that the present test invites "moral mistakes" is difficult to understand. The majority opinion concedes that some individuals cannot conform their conduct to the law's requirements. . . . [T]he majority embraces a rule certain to result in the conviction of at least some who are not morally responsible and the punishment of those for whom retributive, deterrent, and rehabilitative penal goals are inappropriate. A decision that virtually ensures undeserved, and therefore unjust, punishment in the name of avoiding moral mistakes rests on a peculiar notion of morality. . . .

Judges are not, and should not be, immune to popular outrage over this nation's crime rate. Like everyone else, judges watch television, read newspapers and magazines, listen to gossip, and are sometimes themselves victims. They receive the message trenchantly described in a recent book criticizing the insanity defense: "Perhaps the bottom line of all these complaints is that *guilty people go free*. . . . These are not cases in which the defendant is *alleged* to have committed a crime. *Everyone knows he did it*."[25] Although understandable as an expression of uninformed popular opinion, such a viewpoint ought not to serve as the basis for judicial decisionmaking; for it misapprehends the very meaning of guilt.

. . . By definition, guilt cannot be attributed to an individual unable to refrain from violating the law. When a defendant is properly acquit-

25. W. Winslade & J. Ross, The Insanity Plea 2-3 (1983) (emphasis added).

ted by reason of insanity under the control test, the guilty does not go free. . . .

NOTE

The acquittal of John Hinckley, following his attempted assassination of President Reagan, has provoked considerable ferment with respect to the definition and administration of the insanity defense. One trend, illustrated by the *Lyons* decision, has been to narrow the scope of the defense, particularly by eliminating the volitional prong of the test. Courts, legislatures and reform groups have also sought other devices to restrict what are perceived as the undesirable effects of defenses based on mental illness. These other devices are, for doctrinal purposes, examined separately in the Casebook and in the corresponding pages of this Supplement, though they are all, to a degree, designed to respond to the same underlying problem.[a] The present Note focuses on developments with respect to the insanity test itself.

1. *Federal law.* As part of the Comprehensive Crime Control Act of 1984, Congress enacted a provision that supercedes the *Lyons* decision and appears to represent an even greater narrowing of the insanity test. Section 402(a) of the act adds to the United States Code a new provision, 18 U.S.C. §20(a), as follows:

§20. INSANITY DEFENSE

(a) *Affirmative Defense.* It is an affirmative defense to a prosecution under any Federal statute that, at the time of the commission of the acts constituting the offense, the defendant, as a result of a severe mental disease or defect, was unable to appreciate the nature and quality or the wrongfulness of his acts. Mental disease or defect does not otherwise constitute a defense.

2. *California law.* California Penal Code §25(b), adopted by voter initiative in 1982, provides as follows:

In any criminal proceeding, including any juvenile court proceeding, in which a plea of not guilty by reason of insanity is entered, this defense shall be found by the trier of fact only when the accused person proves by a preponderance of the evidence that he or she was incapable of knowing or

a. Developments in the following related areas should be considered: (1) the burden of proof—Casebook pages 842-843 and this Supplement page 89 infra; (2) disposition of insanity acquittees—Casebook pages 843-854 and this Supplement pages 90-102 infra; (3) the verdict of guilty but mentally ill—Casebook pages 854-855 and this Supplement page 102 infra; (4) diminished capacity—Casebook pages 863-878 and this Supplement pages 102-104 infra; and (5) complete abolition of the insanity defense—Casebook pages 901-909 and this Supplement pages 104-105 infra.

understanding the nature and quality of his or her and[a] of distinguishing right from wrong at the time of the commission of the offense.

3. *Legislative proposals.* Three influential bodies have, in very similar language, proposed retention of the cognitive branch of the Model Penal Code test and rejection of the control branch. See American Bar Association, Criminal Justice Mental Health Standards §7-6.1(a) (approved Feb. 9, 1983); American Psychiatric Association, Statement on the Insanity Defense, 140 Am. J. Psychiatry 6 (1983); National Conf. of Commissioners on Uniform State Laws, Model Insanity Defense and Post-Trial Disposition Act §201 (1984). The ABA standard provides:

A person is not responsible for criminal conduct if, at the time of such conduct, and as a result of mental disease or defect, that person was unable to appreciate the wrongfulness of such conduct.

For further discussion of these issues, see Slovenko, The Insanity Defense in the Wake of *Hinckley*, 14 Rut. L. Rev. (1983).

Page 843. Before "(b) Constitutional requirements" add:

As part of the reaction to the *Hinckley* verdict, see this Supplement page 88 supra, there has been a change in recent years. In about half the states, the defendant now must prove his insanity by a preponderance of the evidence. See H. Rep. No. 98-577, 98th Cong., 1st Sess. 14 (1983). For the federal courts, the question is now governed by 18 U.S.C. §20(b), added by the Comprehensive Crime Control Act of 1984: "The defendant has the burden of proving the defense of insanity by clear and convincing evidence." The ABA recommends that in jurisdictions utilizing a test of insanity that focuses solely on cognitive capacities (such as the ABA's own test, see this Supplement page 89 supra), the prosecution should have the burden of disproving the claim of insanity beyond a reasonable doubt. But because of the more elusive nature of the volitional test of insanity, the ABA recommends that in jurisdictions utilizing the Model Penal Code test, the defendant should have the burden of proving insanity by a preponderance of the evidence. American Bar Association, Criminal Justice Mental Health Standards §7-6.9(b) (approved Feb. 9, 1983).

---

a. Query: What is the effect of the provision's use of the conjunctive *and* in place of the disjunctive *or* used in the traditional *M'Naghten* formulation? For one view see People v. Horn, 158 Cal. App. 3d 1014, 205 Cal. Rptr. 119 (1984). — EDS.

Page 843. Before Benham v. Edwards insert:

JONES v. UNITED STATES

Supreme Court of the United States
103 S. Ct. 3043 (1983)

POWELL, J., delivered the opinion of the Court.

The question presented is whether petitioner, who was committed to a mental hospital upon being acquitted of a criminal offense by reason of insanity, must be released because he has been hospitalized for a period longer than he might have served in prison had he been convicted.

I

In the District of Columbia a criminal defendant may be acquitted by reason of insanity if his insanity is "affirmatively established by a preponderance of the evidence." D.C. Code §24-301(j) (1981). If he successfully invokes the insanity defense, he is committed to a mental hospital. §24-301(d)(1).[2] The statute provides several ways of obtaining release. Within 50 days of commitment the acquittee is entitled to a judicial hearing to determine his eligibility for release, at which he has the burden of proving by a preponderance of the evidence that he is no longer mentally ill or dangerous. §24-301(d)(2).[3] If he fails to meet

2. Section 24-301(d)(1) provides:

> If any person tried upon an indictment or information for an offense raises the defense of insanity and is acquitted solely on the ground that he was insane at the time of its commission, he shall be committed to a hospital for the mentally ill until such time as he is eligible for release pursuant to this subsection or subsection (e).

Under this provision, automatic commitment is permissible only if the defendant himself raised the insanity defense. See H.R. Rep. No. 91-907, p.74 (1970); Lynch v. Overholser, 369 U.S. 705 (1962).

3. Section 24-301(d)(2) provides in relevant part:

> (A) A person confined pursuant to paragraph (1) shall have a hearing, unless waived, within 50 days of his confinement to determine whether he is entitled to release from custody....
>
> (B) If the hearing is not waived, the court shall cause notice of the hearing to be served upon the person, his counsel, and the prosecuting attorney and hold the hearing. Within ten days from the date the hearing was begun, the court shall determine the issues and makefindings of fact and conclusions of law with respect thereto. The person confined shall have the burden of proof. If the court finds by a preponderance of the evidence that the person confined is entitled to his release from custody, either conditional or unconditional, the court shall enter such order as may appear appropriate.

this burden at the 50-day hearing, the committed acquittee subsequently may be released, with court approval, upon certification of his recovery by the hospital chief of service. Alternatively, the acquittee is entitled to a judicial hearing every six months at which he may establish by a preponderance of the evidence that he is entitled to release.

Independent of its provision for the commitment of insanity acquittees, the District of Columbia also has adopted a civil-commitment procedure, under which an individual may be committed upon clear and convincing proof by the Government that he is mentally ill and likely to injure himself or others. The individual may demand a jury in the civil-commitment proceeding. Once committed, a patient may be released at any time upon certification of recovery by the hospital chief of service. Alternatively, the patient is entitled after the first 90 days, and subsequently at 6-month intervals, to request a judicial hearing at which he may gain his release by proving by a preponderance of the evidence that he is no longer mentally ill or dangerous.

II

On September 19, 1975, petitioner was arrested for attempting to steal a jacket from a department store. The next day he was arraigned in the District of Columbia Superior Court on a charge of attempted petit larceny, a misdemeanor punishable by a maximum prison sentence of one year. The court ordered petitioner committed to St. Elizabeths, a public hospital for the mentally ill, for a determination of his competency to stand trial. On March 2, 1976, a hospital psychologist submitted a report to the court stating that petitioner was competent to stand trial, that petitioner suffered from "Schizophrenia, paranoid type," and that petitioner's alleged offense was "the product of his mental disease." The court ruled that petitioner was competent to stand trial. Petitioner subsequently decided to plead not guilty by reason of insanity. The Government did not contest the plea, and it entered into a stipulation of facts with petitioner. On March 12, 1976, the Superior Court found petitioner not guilty by reason of insanity and committed him to St. Elizabeths pursuant to §24-301(d)(1).

On May 25, 1976, the court held the 50-day hearing required by

---

The statute does not specify the standard for determining release, but the District of Columbia Court of Appeals held in this case that, as in release proceedings under §24-301(e) and §21-545(b), the confined person must show that he is either no longer mentally ill or no longer dangerous to himself or others. See 432 A.2d 364, 372 and n.16 (1981) (en banc).

§24-301(d)(2)(A). A psychologist from St. Elizabeths testified on behalf of the Government that, in the opinion of the staff, petitioner continued to suffer from paranoid schizophrenia and that "because his illness is still quite active, he is still a danger to himself and to others." Petitioner's counsel conducted a brief cross-examination, and presented no evidence. The court then found that "the defendant-patient is mentally ill and as a result of his mental illness, at this time, he constitutes a danger to himself or others." Petitioner was returned to St. Elizabeths. Petitioner obtained new counsel and, following some procedural confusion, a second release hearing was held on February 22, 1977. By that date petitioner had been hospitalized for more than one year, the maximum period he could have spent in prison if he had been convicted. On [this] basis he demanded that he be released unconditionally or recommitted pursuant to the civil-commitment standards in §21-545(b), including a jury trial and proof by clear and convincing evidence of his mental illness and dangerousness. The Superior Court denied petitioner's request for a civil-commitment hearing, reaffirmed the findings made at the May 25, 1976, hearing, and continued petitioner's commitment to St. Elizabeths.

Petitioner appealed to the District of Columbia Court of Appeals. . . . The Court of Appeals rejected the argument "that the length of the prison sentence [petitioner] might have received determines when he is entitled to release or civil commitment under Title 24 of the D.C. Code."

We granted certiorari and now affirm.

III

It is clear that "commitment for any purpose constitutes a significant deprivation of liberty that requires due process protection." Addington v. Texas, 441 U.S. 418, 425 (1979). Therefore, a State must have "a constitutionally adequate purpose for the confinement." O'Connor v. Donaldson, 422 U.S. 563, 574 (1975). Congress has determined that a criminal defendant found not guilty by reason of insanity in the District of Columbia should be committed indefinitely to a mental institution for treatment and the protection of society. Petitioner does not contest the Government's authority to commit a mentally ill and dangerous person indefinitely to a mental institution, but rather contends that "the petitioner's trial was not a constitutionally adequate hearing to justify an indefinite commitment."

Petitioner's argument rests principally on Addington v. Texas, supra, in which the Court held that the Due Process Clause requires the Government in a civil-commitment proceeding to demonstrate by clear and convincing evidence that the individual is mentally ill and dangerous. Petitioner contends that these due process standards were not met in his case because the judgment of not guilty by reason of insanity did not constitute a finding of present mental illness and dangerousness and because it was established only by a preponderance of the evidence. Petitioner then concludes that the Government's only conceivably legitimate justification for automatic commitment is to ensure that insanity acquittees do not escape confinement entirely, and that this interest can justify commitment at most for a period equal to the maximum prison sentence the acquittee could have received if convicted. Because petitioner has been hospitalized for longer than the one year he might have served in prison, he asserts that he should be released unconditionally or recommitted under the District's civil-commitment procedures.[11]

We turn first to the question whether the finding of insanity at the criminal trial is sufficiently probative of mental illness and dangerousness to justify commitment. A verdict of not guilty by reason of insanity establishes two facts: (i) the defendant committed an act that constitutes a criminal offense, and (ii) he committed the act because of mental illness. Congress has determined that these findings constitute an adequate basis for hospitalizing the acquittee as a dangerous and mentally ill person. See H.R. Rep. No. 91-907, supra, at 74 (expressing fear that "dangerous criminals, particularly psychopaths, [may] win acquittals of serious criminal charges on grounds of insanity" and yet "escape hospital commitment"); S. Rep. No. 1170, 84th Cong., 1st Sess. 13 (1955) ("Where [the] accused has pleaded insanity as a defense to a crime, and the jury has found that the defendant was, in fact, insane at the time the crime was committed, it is just and reasonable in the Committee's

---

11. It is important to note what issues are not raised in this case. Petitioner has not sought appellate review of the Superior Court's findings in 1976 and 1977 that he remained mentally ill and dangerous, and, indeed, the record does not indicate that since 1977 he ever has sought a release hearing—a hearing to which he was entitled every six months.

Nor are we asked to decide whether the District's procedures for release are constitutional. As noted above, the basic standard for release is the same under either civil commitment or commitment following acquittal by reason of insanity: the individual must prove by a preponderance of the evidence that he is no longer dangerous or mentally ill. There is an important difference, however, in the release provisions for these two groups. A patient who is committed civilly is entitled to unconditional release upon certification of his recovery by the hospital chief of service, whereas a committed insanity acquittee may be released upon such certification only with court approval. Neither of these provisions is before the Court, as petitioner has challenged neither the adequacy of the release standards generally nor the disparity in treatment of insanity acquittees and other committed persons.

opinion that the insanity, once established, should be presumed to continue and that the accused should automatically be confined for treatment until it can be shown that he has recovered"). We cannot say that it was unreasonable and therefore unconstitutional for Congress to make this determination.

The fact that a person has been found, beyond a reasonable doubt, to have committed a criminal act certainly indicates dangerousness. Indeed, this concrete evidence generally may be at least as persuasive as any predictions about dangerousness that might be made in a civil-commitment proceeding.[13] We do not agree with petitioner's suggestion that the requisite dangerousness is not established by proof that a person committed a non-violent crime against property. This Court never has held that "violence," however that term might be defined, is a prerequisite for a constitutional commitment.[14]

Nor can we say that it was unreasonable for Congress to determine that the insanity acquittal supports an inference of continuing mental illness. It comports with common sense to conclude that someone whose mental illness was sufficient to lead him to commit a criminal act is likely to remain ill and in need of treatment. The precise evidentiary force of the insanity acquittal, of course, may vary from case to case, but the Due Process Clause does not require Congress to make classifications that fit every individual with the same degree of relevance.

13. In attacking the predictive value of the insanity acquittal, petitioner complains that "[w]hen Congress enacted the present statutory scheme, it did not cite any empirical evidence indicating that mentally ill persons who have committed a criminal act are likely to commit additional dangerous acts in the future." He further argues that the available research fails to support the predictive value of prior dangerous acts. We do not agree with the suggestion that Congress' power to legislate in this area depends on the research conducted by the psychiatric community. . . .

14. See Overholser v. O'Beirne, 112 App. D.C. 267, 302 F.2d 852, 861 (1961) (Burger, J.) ("[T]o describe the theft of watches and jewelry as 'non-dangerous' is to confuse danger with violence. Larceny is usually less violent than murder or assault, but in terms of public policy the purpose of the statute is the same as to both.") (footnote omitted). It also may be noted that crimes of theft frequently may result in violence from the efforts of the criminal to escape or the victim to protect property or the police to apprehend the fleeing criminal.

The relative "dangerousness" of a particular individual, of course, should be a consideration at the release hearings. In this context, it is noteworthy that petitioner's continuing commitment may well rest in significant part on evidence independent of his acquittal by reason of insanity of the crime of attempted larceny. In December 1976 a medical officer at St. Elizabeths reported that petitioner "has a history of attempted suicide." In addition, petitioner at one point was transferred to the civil division of the hospital, but was transferred back to the forensic division because of disruptive behavior. The Government also advises that after petitioner was released unconditionally following the second panel decision below, he had to be recommitted on an emergency civil basis two weeks later for conduct unrelated to the original commitment.

Because a hearing is provided within 50 days of the commitment, there is assurance that every acquittee has prompt opportunity to obtain release if he has recovered.

Petitioner also argues that, whatever the evidentiary value of the insanity acquittal, the Government lacks a legitimate reason for committing insanity acquittees automatically because it can introduce the insanity acquittal as evidence in a subsequent civil proceeding. This argument fails to consider the Government's strong interest in avoiding the need to conduct a de novo commitment hearing following every insanity acquittal—a hearing at which a jury trial may be demanded, §21-544, and at which the Government bears the burden of proof by clear and convincing evidence. Instead of focusing on the critical question whether the acquittee has recovered, the new proceeding likely would have to relitigate much of the criminal trial. These problems accent the Government's important interest in automatic commitment. See Mathews v. Eldridge, 424 U.S. 319, 348 (1976). We therefore conclude that a finding of not guilty by reason of insanity is a sufficient foundation for commitment of an insanity acquittee for the purposes of treatment and the protection of society.

Petitioner next contends that his indefinite commitment is unconstitutional because the proof of his insanity was based only on a preponderance of the evidence, as compared to Addington's civil-commitment requirement of proof by clear and convincing evidence. In equating these situations, petitioner ignores important differences between the class of potential civil-commitment candidates and the class of insanity acquittees that justify differing standards of proof. The Addington Court expressed particular concern that members of the public could be confined on the basis of "some abnormal behavior which might be perceived by some as symptomatic of a mental or emotional disorder, but which is in fact within a range of conduct that is generally acceptable." In view of this concern, the Court deemed it inappropriate to ask the individual "to share equally with society the risk of error." But since automatic commitment under §24-301(d)(1) follows only if the *acquittee himself* advances insanity as a defense and proves that his criminal act was a product of his mental illness, there is good reason for diminished concern as to the risk of error. More important, the proof that he committed a criminal act as a result of mental illness eliminates the risk that he is being committed for mere "idiosyncratic behavior," *Addington*, 441 U.S., at 427. A criminal act by definition is not "within a range of conduct that is generally acceptable."

We therefore conclude that concerns critical to our decision in *Addington* are diminished or absent in the case of insanity acquittees. Accordingly, there is no reason for adopting the same standard of proof in both cases. . . . The preponderance of the evidence standard comports with due process for commitment of insanity acquittees.[17]

The remaining question is whether petitioner nonetheless is entitled to his release because he has been hospitalized for a period longer than he could have been incarcerated if convicted. The Due Process Clause "requires that the nature and duration of commitment bear some reasonable relation to the purpose for which the individual is committed." Jackson v. Indiana, 406 U.S. 715, 738 (1972). The purpose of commitment following an insanity acquittal, like that of civil commitment, is to treat the individual's mental illness and protect him and society from his potential dangerousness. . . . And because it is impossible to predict how long it will take for any given individual to recover—or indeed whether he ever will recover—Congress has chosen, as it has with respect to civil commitment, to leave the length of commitment indeterminate, subject to periodic review of the patient's suitability for release.

In light of the congressional purposes underlying commitment of insanity acquittees, we think petitioner clearly errs in contending that an acquittee's hypothetical maximum sentence provides the constitutional limit for his commitment. A particular sentence of incarceration is chosen to reflect society's view of the proper response to commission of a particular criminal offense, based on a variety of considerations such as retribution, deterrence, and rehabilitation. The State may punish a person convicted of a crime even if satisfied that he is unlikely to commit further crimes.

Different considerations underlie commitment of an insanity acquittee. As he was not convicted, he may not be punished. His confinement rests on his continuing illness and dangerousness. Thus, under the District of Columbia statute, no matter how serious the act committed by the acquittee, he may be released within 50 days of his acquittal if he has recovered. In contrast, one who committed a less serious act may be confined for a longer period if he remains ill and dangerous. There simply is no necessary correlation between severity of the offense and length of time necessary for recovery. The length of the acquittee's

17. A defendant could be required to prove his insanity by a higher standard than a preponderance of the evidence. See Leland v. Oregon, 343 U.S. 790 (1952). Such an additional requirement hardly would benefit a criminal defendant who wants to raise the insanity defense, yet imposition of a higher standard would be a likely legislative response to a holding that an insanity acquittal could support automatic commitment only if the verdict were supported by clear and convincing evidence.

hypothetical criminal sentence therefore is irrelevant to the purposes of his commitment.[19]

IV

We hold that when a criminal defendant establishes by a preponderance of the evidence that he is not guilty of a crime by reason of insanity, the Constitution permits the Government, on the basis of the insanity judgment, to confine him to a mental institution until such time as he has regained his sanity or is no longer a danger to himself or society. This holding accords with the widely and reasonably held view that insanity acquittees constitute a special class that should be treated differently from other candidates for commitment.[20] . . .

The judgment of the District of Columbia Court of Appeals is affirmed.

BRENNAN, J., with whom MARSHALL and BLACKMUN, JJ., join, dissenting.

The Court begins by posing the wrong question. The issue in this case is not whether petitioner must be released because he has been hospitalized for longer than the prison sentence he might have served had he been convicted, any more than the question in a motion to suppress an allegedly coerced confession at a murder trial is whether the murderer should go free. The question before us is whether the

19. . . . The inherent fallacy of relying on a criminal sanction to determine the length of a therapeutic confinement is manifested by petitioner's failure to suggest any clear guidelines for deciding when a patient must be released. For example, he does not suggest whether the Due Process Clause would require States to limit commitment of insanity acquittees to maximum sentences or minimum sentences. Nor does he explain what should be done in the case of indeterminate sentencing or suggest whether account would have to be taken of the availability of release time or the possibility of parole. And petitioner avoids entirely the important question how this theory would apply to those persons who committed especially serious criminal acts. Petitioner thus would leave the States to speculate how they may deal constitutionally with acquittees who might have received life imprisonment, life imprisonment without possibility of parole, or the death penalty.

20. A recent survey of commitment statutes reported that 14 jurisdictions provide automatic commitment for at least some insanity acquittees, while many other States have a variety of special methods of committing insanity acquittees. See Note, Commitment Following an Insanity Acquittal, 94 Harv. L. Rev. 605, 605-606, and nn. 4-6 (1981). Nineteen States commit insanity acquittees under the same procedures used for civil commitment. Id., at 605, n.3. It appears that only one State has enacted into law petitioner's suggested requirement that a committed insanity acquittee be released following expiration of his hypothetical maximum criminal sentence. See Conn. Gen. Stat. §53a-47(b) (Supp. 1981).

fact that an individual has been found "not guilty by reason of insanity," by itself, provides a constitutionally adequate basis for involuntary, indefinite commitment to psychiatric hospitalization. . . .

The obvious difference between insanity acquittees and other candidates for civil commitment is that, at least in the District of Columbia, an acquittal by reason of insanity implies a determination beyond a reasonable doubt that the defendant in fact committed the criminal act with which he was charged. Conceivably, the Government may have an interest in confining insanity acquittees to punish them for their criminal acts, but the Government disclaims any such interest, and the Court does not rely on it. . . . [4]

Instead of relying on a punishment rationale, the Court holds that a finding of insanity at a criminal trial "is sufficiently probative of mental illness and dangerousness to justify commitment." . . .

Our precedents in other commitment contexts are inconsistent with the argument that the mere facts of past criminal behavior and mental illness justify indefinite commitment without the benefits of the minimum due process standards associated with civil commitment, most importantly proof of present mental illness and dangerousness by clear and convincing evidence. . . .

The petitioner in Baxstrom [v. Herold, 383 U.S. 107 (1966)] had been convicted of assault and sentenced to a term in prison, during which he was certified as insane by a prison physician. At the expiration of his criminal sentence, he was committed involuntarily to a state mental hospital under procedures substantially less protective than those used for civil commitment. We held that, once he had served his sentence, Baxstrom could not be treated differently from other candidates for civil commitment. . . .

The Government's interests in committing petitioner are the same interests involved in *Addington* [and] *Baxstrom* . . . — isolation, protection, and treatment of a person who may, through no fault of his own, cause harm to others or to himself. Whenever involuntary commitment is a possibility, the Government has a strong interest in accurate, effi-

---

4. Punishing someone acquitted by reason of insanity would undoubtedly implicate important constitutional concerns. It is questionable that confinement to a mental hospital would pass constitutional muster as appropriate punishment for any crime. The insanity defense has traditionally been viewed as premised on the notion that society has no interest in punishing insanity acquittees, because they are neither blameworthy nor the appropriate objects of deterrence. See A. Goldstein, The Insanity Defense 15 (1967). In addition, insanity and *mens rea* stand in a close relationship, which this Court has never fully plumbed. See Powell v. Texas, 392 U.S. 514, 536-537 (1968) (opinion of Marshall, J.); Leland v. Oregon, 343 U.S. 790, 800 (1952); cf. Mullaney v. Wilbur, 421 U.S. 684 (1975).

cient commitment decisions. Nevertheless, *Addington* held both that the Government's interest in accuracy was not impaired by a requirement that it bear the burden of persuasion by clear and convincing evidence, and that the individual's interests in liberty and autonomy required the Government to bear at least that burden. An acquittal by reason of insanity of a single, nonviolent misdemeanor is not a constitutionally adequate substitute for the due process protections of *Addington* . . . i.e., proof by clear and convincing evidence of present mental illness or dangerousness, with the Government bearing the burden of persuasion.

A "not guilty by reason of insanity" verdict is backward-looking, focusing on one moment in the past, while commitment requires a judgment as to the present and future. In some jurisdictions, most notably in federal criminal trials, an acquittal by reason of insanity may mean only that a jury found a reasonable doubt as to a defendant's sanity and as to the causal relationship between his mental condition and his crime. See Davis v. United States, 160 U.S. 469 (1985). As we recognized in *Addington,* "the subtleties and nuances of psychiatric diagnosis render certainties virtually beyond reach in most situations." The question is not whether "government may not act in the face of this uncertainty," *ante;* everyone would agree that it can. Rather, the question is whether — in light of the uncertainty about the relationship between petitioner's crime, his present dangerousness, and his present mental condition — the Government can force him for the rest of his life "to share equally with society the risk of error," [*Addington, supra*].

It is worth examining what is known about the possibility of predicting dangerousness from *any* set of facts. Although a substantial body of research suggests that a consistent pattern of violent behavior may, from a purely statistical standpoint, indicate a certain likelihood of further violence in the future, mere statistical validity is far from perfect for purposes of predicting which individuals will be dangerous. Commentators and researchers have long acknowledged that even the best attempts to identify dangerous individuals on the basis of specified facts have been inaccurate roughly two-thirds of the time, almost always on the side of over-prediction. On a clinical basis, mental health professionals can diagnose past or present mental condition with some confidence, but strong institutional biases lead them to err when they attempt to determine an individual's dangerousness, especially when the consequence of a finding of dangerousness is that an obviously mentally ill patient will remain within their control. Research is practically nonexistent on the relationship of *non-violent* criminal behavior, such as petitioner's attempt to shoplift, to future dangerousness. We do not even know whether it is even statistically valid as a predictor of similar non-violent behavior, much less of behavior posing more serious risks to self and others.

Even if an insanity acquittee remains mentally ill, so long as he has not repeated the same act since his offense the passage of time diminishes the likelihood that he will repeat it. Finally, it cannot be gainsaid that some crimes are more indicative of dangerousness than others. . . . [T]here is room for doubt whether a single attempt to shoplift and a string of brutal murders are equally accurate and equally permanent predictors of dangerousness.[13] . . .

. . . Today's decision . . . does not, however, purport to overrule *Baxstrom* or any of the cases which have followed *Baxstrom.* It is clear, therefore, that the separate facts of criminality and mental illness cannot support indefinite psychiatric commitment, for both were present in *Baxstrom.* . . . The Court relies on a *connection* between mental condition and criminal conduct that is unique to verdicts of "not guilty by reason of insanity." Yet the relevance of that connection, as opposed to each of its separate components, is far from a matter of obvious "common sense." None of the available evidence that criminal behavior of the mentally ill is likely to repeat itself distinguishes between behaviors that were "the product"of mental illness and those that were not. It is completely unlikely that persons acquitted by reason of insanity display a rate of future "dangerous" activity higher than civil committees with similar arrest records, or than persons convicted of crimes who are later found to be mentally ill. . . .

Given the close similarity of the governmental interests at issue in this case and those at issue in *Addington,* and the highly imperfect "fit" between the findings required for an insanity acquittal and those required . . . to support an indefinite commitment, I cannot agree that the Government should be excused from the burden that *Addington* held was required by due process.[16] . . .

13. The Court responds that "crimes of theft frequently may result in violence." When they do, that fact may well be relevant to, or even dispositive of the dangerousness issue at a proper commitment hearing. In this case, however, petitioner's attempt to shoplift involved neither actual violence nor any attempt to resist or evade arrest. It is difficult to see how the Court's generalization justifies relieving the Government of its *Addington-O'Connor* burden of proving present dangerousness by clear and convincing evidence.

16. Note that extended institutionalization may effectively make it impossible for an individual to prove that he is no longer mentally ill and dangerous, both because it deprives him of the economic wherewithal to obtain independent medical judgments and because the treatment he receives may make it difficult to demonstrate recovery. The current emphasis on using psychotropic drugs to eliminate the charateristic signs and symptoms of mental illness, especially schizophrenia, may render mental patients docile and unlikely to engage in violent or bizarre behaviors while they are institutionalized; but it does not "cure" them or allow them to demonstrate that they would remain non-violent if they were not drugged.

STEVENS, J., dissenting.

... What Justice Powell has written lends support to the view that the *initial* confinement of the acquittee is permissible, but provides no support for the conclusion that he has the burden of proving his entitlement to freedom after he has served the maximum sentence authorized by law. I respectfully dissent because I believe this shoplifter was presumptively entitled to his freedom after he had been incarcerated for a period of one year.

NOTE

The *Jones* decision explicitly refrains from addressing the validity of Jones's initial commitment and the validity of the District of Columbia procedures for release. Supplement page 93 n. 11, supra. A thorough analysis of due process and equal protection requirements in connection with the initial commitment of insanity acquittees and in connection with procedures for their release appears in Benham v. Edwards, Casebook page 843. *Benham* should be read at this point. The decision was affirmed by the Court of Appeals, 678 F.2d 511 (5th Cir. 1982), and then vacated by the Supreme Court and remanded for further consideration in light of *Jones*. 103 S. Ct. 3565 (1983). How should *Benham* be decided on remand?

Page 849. After "Notes and Questions," replace "1. Other judicial approaches" with the following new note:

1. The Comprehensive Crime Control Act of 1984 adds to the United States Code a new provision, 18 U.S.C. §4243, providing for hospitalization of insanity acquittees. After requiring an initial commitment for observation and examination, the statute requires a hearing to determine whether the acquittee should be released. Section 4243(d) provides that at such a hearing:

> a person found not guilty only by reason of insanity of an offense involving bodily injury to, or serious damage to the property of, another person, or involving a substantial risk of such injury or damage, has the burden of proving by clear and convincing evidence that his release would not create a substantial risk of bodily injury to another person or serious damage of property of another due to a present mental disease or defect. With respect to any other offense, the person has the burden of such proof of a preponderance of the evidence.

If the acquittee is committed after the initial hearing, then in any subsequent proceeding he must satisfy the burden of proof specified in

§4243(d) in order to obtain his release. See §4243(f). Questions: Are these burden of proof provisions constitutional? Are they justified by the Court's reasoning in *Jones?*

Page 855. Before "3. Questions" insert:

For further discussion of the verdict of "guilty but mentally ill," see Taylor v. State, 440 N.E.2d 1109 (Ind. 1982) (rejecting a constitutional challenge); Note, The Guilty But Mentally Ill Verdict and Due Process, 92 Yale L.J. 475 (1983).

Page 865. Before the last full paragraph on the page add:

For a helpful discussion of the English experience, see Dell, Diminished Responsibility Reconsidered, [1982] Crim. L. Rev. 809.

Page 866. Before Bethea v. United States insert:

For further criticism of psychiatric evidence in criminal trials, see Morse, Undiminished Confusion in Diminished Capacity, 75 J. Crim. L. & C. 1 (1984); Morse, Failed Explanations and Criminal Responsibility: Experts and the Unconscious, 68 Va. L. Rev. 971 (1982). For a different view, see Bonnie & Slobogin, The Role of Mental Health Professionals in the Criminal Process: The Case for Informed Speculation, 66 Va. L. Rev. 427 (1980).

Page 871. Before "2. Constitutional issues" insert:

Adding to the confusion is §25 of the California Penal Code, adopted pursuant to voter initiative in 1982:

> (a) The defense of diminished capacity is hereby abolished. In a criminal action, as well as any juvenile court proceeding, evidence concerning an accused person's intoxication, trauma, mental illness, disease, or defect shall not be admissible to show or negate capacity to form the particular purpose, intent, motive, malice aforethought, knowledge, or other mental state required for the commission of the crime charged.
>
> (b) [For the text of this subsection see this Supplement pages 88-89 supra.]
>
> (c) Notwithstanding the foregoing, evidence of diminished capacity or of mental disorder may be considered by the court only at the time of the sentencing or other disposition or commitment.

Note that these provisions do not expressly repeal §28 (Casebook page 870) and that the legislature enacted some minor stylistic changes to §28 in 1984. What is the effect of §§25 (a) & (c) on the second sentence of §28(a)?

Page 871. At the bottom of the page insert:

In Muensch v. Israel, 715 F.2d 1124 (7th Cir. 1983), the court of appeals upheld the constitutionality of state murder convictions at trials in which the defendants were precluded from introducing psychiatric evidence of their abnormal personalities in order to prove that they lacked the capacity to form an intent to kill. Hughes v. Matthews, Casebook page 871, was distinguished on the following grounds (715 F.2d at 1137, 1144):

> In *Hughes* we determined that when evidence is considered relevant and competent under state law, a criminal defendant may not be precluded from presenting it in his defense if the *policy* considerations advanced in support of exclusion are inapplicable in the context of the situation. We took pains in *Hughes* to point out that we were not seeking to constitutionalize the law of evidence nor to impose a diminished responsibility doctrine on Wisconsin. Yet that is just what petitioners in the instant case seek: they argue that they have a constitutional right to present psychiatric evidence of their abnormal personalities in order to prove that they lacked the capacity to form an intent to kill. This contention is not a new one. In fact, it has been rejected by the Supreme Court of the United States on several occasions. . . .
>
> The essential flaw in petitioners' argument is that the basic fact which they wish to establish is that they suffered from a personality disorder. It is not disputed that experts in psychology are competent to testify regarding that basic fact. What is the dispute—indeed, the entire debate over the doctrine of diminished capacity has as its focal point—is whether a personality disorder is probative of the defendant's capacity to form an intent to kill. Petitioners' experts contended that personality disorders rendered them unable to form such an intent. That is, their experts contended that the fact of their personality disorders was a material issue in their cases because the fact was probative of whether they were capable of entertaining a mental state in issue. In short, petitioners essentially maintain that the psychiatric testimony they proffered is relevant because their witnesses said so. The proposition does not survive its statement.

Judge Cudahy, dissenting, observed (715 F.2d at 1145-1147):

> [O]ur understanding of early Supreme Court precedent must be informed by the subsequent Supreme Court decisions in Washington v. Texas, 388 U.S. 14 (1967), and Chambers v. Mississippi, 410 U.S. 284 (1973). In both *Washington* and *Chambers*, the Court broke new ground in evaluating state evidentiary rules that exclude evidence offered by criminal defendants. At the very least, these cases hold that a state may not arbitrarily or mechanistically define the uses to which relevant and competent evidence may be put. . . .
>
> . . . [T]he state's assertion that it must exclude *expert* testimony on the defendant's mens rea lest this testimony interfere with the jury's determination of specific intent to kill seems inconsistent with its willingness to allow

the jury to hear all manner of testimony on the very same subject without any expert component. . . .

. . . [A]lthough the state asserted a distinction between expert testimony on mens rea capacity and expert testimony with respect to insanity, the Wisconsin Supreme Court also made the point that the former sort of testimony was "substantially congruent with evidence supportive of the . . . test for insanity to be utilized in the second phase of the bifurcated trial. . . . Both tests focus on exactly the same mental defect—lack of capacity." But this observation seems to suggest that insanity and mens rea incapacity are merely labels for the same disorganization of mind and personality; therefore, the evidentiary analysis with respect to one may very well virtually duplicate the analysis of the other. . . .

Therefore, I find the state's justifications for its position unpersuasive and, on the basis of *Hughes, Chambers* and *Washington,* I would grant the writs.

Page 903. At the end of the Note add:

In State v. Korell, 690 P.2d 992 (Mont. 1984), the Montana Supreme Court upheld the constitutionality of that state's legislation abolishing the insanity defense. The court stressed that, unlike the statute at issue in *Strasburg,* see Casebook page 902, the Montana legislation expressly allows evidence of mental disease or defect to be introduced to rebut evidence offered to prove that the defendant had the required mens rea. The court conceded that this approach would still lead to the conviction of a defendant who, like Korell himself, did formulate an intent to cause harm but did so under the influence of a mental disease that produced a completely deluded perception of reality or a lack of volitional control. The court held, however, that the provisions requiring hospitalization after conviction in such a case served to avoid cruel and unusual punishment. In response to the argument that the statutory scheme still violated fundamental principles of justice, because the defendant in such a case still suffered the stigma of criminal conviction (and the prospect of incarceration in prison if his mental disease was pronounced cured before the expiration of his sentence), the court answered:

> We cannot agree. The legislature has made a conscious decision to hold individuals who act with a proven criminal state of mind accountable for their acts, regardless of motivation or mental condition. Arguably, this policy does not further criminal justice goals of deterrence and prevention in cases where an accused suffers from a mental disease that renders him incapable of appreciating the criminality of his conduct. However, the policy does further goals of protection of society and education. One State Supreme Court Justice who wrestled with this dilemma observed: "In a very real sense, the confinement of the insane is the punishment of the innocent;

the release of the insane is the punishment of society." State v. Stacy (Tenn. 1980), 601 S.W.2d 696, 704 (Henry, J., dissenting).

For further consideration of the constitutionality and desirability of abolishing the insanity defense, see the materials that follow, Casebook pages 904-909 and this Supplement page 105 infra.

Page 909. Between the first and second paragraphs of Note 3 insert:

The American Medical Association has formally proposed that the insanity defense as such be abolished and that evidence of the defendant's mental disease or defect be admissible solely on the issue of whether he possessed the mens rea of the crime charged. See 34 Crim. L. Rptr. 2228 (Dec. 21, 1983). For a thoughtful defense of a similar position, see N. Morris, Madness and the Criminal Law (1982). The ABA, in contrast, has explicitly rejected this approach; the ABA concluded that "[s]uch a jarring reversal of hundreds of years of moral and legal history would constitute an unfortunate and unwarranted overreaction to the *Hinckley* verdict." ABA Standing Committee on Association Standards for Criminal Justice, Report to the House of Delegates, Commentary on Standard 7-6.1, p. 327 (Aug. 1984).

Chapter Ten
Theft Offenses

Page 919. Before Topolewski v. State insert:

Defendant removed a price label for £2.73 from a piece of meat in a supermarket and affixed the label to a piece of meat that should have cost £6.91. His act was detected at the checkout counter before he paid for the second piece of meat. Could the defendant be convicted of common law larceny? Could he be convicted under a statute like Model Penal Code §223.2(1), which makes liability turn on the question whether the defendant has "exercise[d] unlawful control"? In any event could the defendant be convicted of attempted theft? See Anderton v. Burnside (House of Lords, 1983), reported and commented on in [1983] Crim. L. Rev. 813.

Page 966. At the end of the first paragraph of Note 2 insert:

The Seventh Circuit has explicitly rejected both the reasoning and the result in the *Chappell* case. United States v. Croft, 750 F.2d 1354 (7th Cir. 1984).

Page 986. At the end of the Note add:

The federal extortion statute, the Hobbs Act, 18 U.S.C. §1951, was patterned on New York law as it stood at the time of the *Fichtner* decision. As a result, the federal courts have rejected the position reflected in *Butler*, Casebook page 981, and in Model Penal Code §223.1(3), Casebook page 983; instead they have held, in accord with *Fichtner*, that a claim of right is no defense to a charge of extortion under the Hobbs Act. See, e.g., United States v. Agnes, 36 Crim. L. Rptr. 2354 (3d Cir., Jan.24, 1985).

Chapter Eleven
Business Crimes

Page 1006. At the end of the carryover paragraph add:

5. A recent article argues that some of the payments prohibited by the FCPA are morally permissible. Carson, Bribery, Extortion, and the Foreign Corrupt Practices Act, 15 Phil. & Pub. Affairs 66 (1985).

Page 1006. Before "1. Liability of the Corporate Entity" insert:

For a useful overview of these problems, see Brickey, Corporate Criminal Liability: A Primer for Corporate Counsel, 40 Bus. Law. 129 (1984).

Page 1014. Before Note 4 insert:

For further discussion of these issues, see Fisse, Reconstructing Corporate Criminal Law: Deterence, Retribution, Fault, and Sanctions, 56 So. Cal. L. Rev. 1141 (1983); Note, Economic Inefficiency of Corporate Criminal Liability, 73 J. Crim. L. & C. 582 (1982).

Page 1033. At the end of Note 3 add:

4. Useful discussion of the issues raised by the *Park* case may be found in Abrams, Criminal Liability of Corporate Officers for Strict Liability Offenses — A Comment on *Dotterweich* and *Park*, 28 U.C.L.A.L. Rev. 463 (1981); Brickey, Criminal Liability of Corporate Officers for Strict Liability — Another View, 35 Vand. L. Rev. 1337 (1982).

Chapter Twelve

Disposition of Convicted Offenders

Page 1058. In note a, delete subsections (2) and (3) of Rule 32(c) and replace by the following:

(2) Report. The presentence report shall contain —

(A) any prior criminal record of the defendant;

(B) a statement of the circumstances of the commission of the offense and circumstances affecting the defendant's behavior;

(C) information concerning any harm, including financial, social, psychological, and physical harm, done to or loss suffered by any victim of the offense; and

(D) any other information that may aid the court in sentencing, including the restitution needs of any victim of the offense.

(3) Disclosure.

(A) At a reasonable time before imposing sentence the court shall permit the defendant and his counsel to read the report of the presentence investigation exclusive of any recommendation as to sentence, but not to the extent that in the opinion of the court the report contains diagnostic opinions which, if disclosed, might seriously disrupt a program of rehabilitation; or sources of information obtained upon a promise of confidentiality; or any other information which, if disclosed, might result in harm, physical or otherwise, to the defendant or other persons. The court shall afford the defendant and his counsel an opportunity to comment on the report and, in the discretion of the court, to introduce testimony or other information relating to any alleged factual inaccuracy contained in it.

(B) If the court is of the view that there is information in the presentence report which should not be disclosed under subdivision (c)(3)(A) of this rule, the court in lieu of making the report or part thereof available shall state orally or in writing a summary of the factual information contained therein to be relied on in determining sentence, and shall give the defendant and his counsel an opportunity to comment thereon. The statement may be made to the parties in camera.

(C) Any material which may be disclosed to the defendant and his counsel shall be disclosed to the attorney for the government.

(D) If the comments of the defendant and his counsel or testimony or other information introduced by them allege any factual inaccuracy in the presentence investigation report or the summary of the report or part thereof, the court shall, as to each matter controverted, make (i) a finding as to the allegation, or (ii) a determination that no such finding is necessary because the matter controverted will not be taken into account in sentencing. A written record of such findings and determinations shall be appended to and accompany any copy of the presentence investigation report thereafter made available to the Bureau of Prisons or the Parole Commission.

(E) Any copies of the presentence investigation report made available to the defendant and his counsel and the attorney for the government shall be returned to the probation officer immediately following the imposition of sentence or the granting of probation, unless the court, in its discretion, otherwise directs.

(F) The reports of studies and recommendations contained therein made by the Director of the Bureau of Prisons or the Parole Commission pursuant to 18 U.S.C. §§4205(c), 4252, 5010(e), or 5037(c) shall be considered a presentence investigation within the meaning of subdivision (c)(3) of this rule.

Note that the Sentencing Reform Act of 1984 makes a number of changes in Rule 32(c) that will take effect on November 1, 1986. The changes serve to bring Rule 32(c) into conformity with the new guidelines sentencing system (see this Supplement pages 114-115 infra), principally by deleting references to the Parole Commission, and by specifying that the report prepared pursuant to Rule 32(c)(2) shall include the information necessary for application of the appropriate guidelines and policy statements issued by the new United States Sentencing Commission.

Page 1059. At the end of the Note insert:

The revised language of Rule 32(c)(3), see this Supplement pages 111-112 supra, was adopted in 1982 and 1983, in large measure as a response to the findings of the Fennell & Hall study (Casebook page 1059). The new wording is intended to assure that counsel obtains access to the report without request and under circumstances that afford a reasonable opportunity for effective review of the report. For discussion see United States v. Rone, 36 Crim. L. Rptr. 2013 (7th Cir., Sept. 4, 1984).

Page 1069. Before the first paragraph of the Note insert:

In an important recent decision, the Michigan Supreme Court, without awaiting legislative reform, used its own judicial authority to institute a system of appellate review of sentences. See People v. Coles, 417 Mich. 523, 339 N.W.2d 440 (1983).

Page 1076. Before "5. Parole" insert the following new note:

3. The Sentencing Reform Act of 1984 adds to the United States Code a new section, 18 U.S.C. §3742, which provides for appellate review of sentences in federal criminal cases. Both the defendant and the prosecution are authorized to appeal. The court of appeals may either decrease or increase the sentence, if it finds that the sentence imposed was "unreasonable," but the court may order an increase only when the prosecution has appealed.

Page 1106. After Question 3 add:

NOTE

In Mabry v. Johnson, 104 S. Ct. 2543 (1984), the Court expressly rejected the holding in the *Cooper* case (Casebook page 1101). Writing for a unanimous Court, Justice Stevens said that "only when it develops that the defendant was not fairly apprised of its consequences can his plea be challenged under the Due Process Clause." 104 S. Ct. at 2547. Thus, when the prosecutor reneges on a plea offer after the defendant has accepted it, and the defendant subsequently accepts a second, less favorable offer, the defendant's plea does not, as in *Santobello* (Casebook page 1096), rest on a false premise or a deceptive inducement. Rather, the plea, under the terms of the subsequent offer, satisfies all constitutional requirements of a voluntary, intelligent waiver. The Court held that it was irrelevant whether the prosecutor had been negligent or otherwise culpable in making and then withdrawing the first offer; "[t]he Due Process Clause is not a code of ethics for prosecutors." 104 S. Ct. at 2548. Finally, the notion that the withdrawal of the first offer might somehow undermine the defendant's Sixth Amendment right to counsel (see *Cooper*, Casebook pages 1103-1104 & n.9) was dismissed as "simply at odds with reason." 104 S. Ct. at 2548 n.10.

Page 1120. At the bottom of the page add:

NOTE

The Sentencing Reform Act of 1984 amends the United States Code to provide for the creation of a United States Sentencing Commission, 28 U.S.C. §§991-998. The act states, 28 U.S.C. §991(b)(2), that the purpose of the commission is to establish sentencing policies that will both serve the purposes of sentencing (as defined in 18 U.S.C. §3553(a)(2), set out below) and also "provide certainty and fairness . . . [and avoid] unwarranted sentencing disparities." To this end, the Commission is directed in 28 U.S.C. §994(a)(1) to promulgate guidelines for use by the sentencing judge in determining the sentence to be imposed in federal criminal cases. The guideline ranges must be relatively narrow; for sentences of imprisonment, the maximum of the range may not exceed the minimum by more than 25 percent. See 28 U.S.C. §994(b).

The act also specifies the method that sentencing judges must use to arrive at the appropriate sentence; 18 U.S.C. §3553 provides as follows:

§3553. IMPOSITION OF A SENTENCE

(a) *Factors to be Considered in Imposing a Sentence.* The court shall impose a sentence sufficient, but not greater than necessary, to comply with the purposes set forth in paragraph (2) of this subsection. The court, in determining the particular sentence to be imposed, shall consider—

(1) the nature and circumstances of the offense and the history and characteristics of the defendant;

(2) the need for the sentence imposed—

(A) to reflect the seriousness of the offense, to promote respect for the law, and to provide just punishment for the offense;

(B) to afford adequate deterrence to criminal conduct;

(C) to protect the public from further crimes of the defendant; and

(D) to provide the defendant with needed educational or vocational training, medical care, or other correctional treatment in the most effective manner;

(3) the kinds of sentences available;

(4) the kinds of sentence and the sentencing range established for the applicable category of offense committed by the applicable category of defendant as set forth in the guidelines that are issued by the Sentencing Commission pursuant to 28 U.S.C. 994(a)(1) and that are in effect on the date the defendant is sentenced; . . .

(6) the need to avoid unwarranted sentence disparities among defendants with similar records who have been found guilty of similar conduct.

(b) *Application of Guidelines in Imposing a Sentence.* The court shall impose a sentence of the kind, and within the range, referred to in subsection (a)(4) unless the court finds that an aggravating or mitigating circumstance exists that was not adequately taken into consideration by the Sentencing Commission in formulating the guidelines and that should result in a sentence different from that described.

(c) *Statement of Reasons for Imposing a Sentence.* The court, at the time of sentencing, shall state in open court the reasons for its imposition of the particular sentence, and, if the sentence —

(1) is of the kind, and within the range, described in subsection (a)(4), the reason for imposing a sentence at a particular point within the range; or

(2) is not of the kind, or is outside the range, described in subsection (a)(4), the specific reason for the imposition of a sentence different from that described. . . .

Page 1126. Before "4. Parole" insert:

The federal Sentencing Reform Act of 1984 addresses the plea bargaining problem by requiring the new United States Sentencing Commission to promulgate "policy statements" regarding the appropriate use of the trial judge's authority under F.R. Crim. Pro. 11(e)(2) to accept or reject a plea agreement. See 28 U.S.C. §994(a)(2)(D). The act also requires the judge to consider such policy statements in determining the appropriate sentence. See 18 U.S.C. §3553(a)(5). Presumably, the Commission's policy statements are intended to include guidelines concerning the appropriate scope of charge bargaining, in order to assure uniformity in sentences imposed pursuant to plea agreements. The proposal on which the act's plea bargaining provision was based is set out and explained in 1 S. Schulhofer, Prosecutorial Discretion and Federal Sentencing Reform 114-132 (Federal Judicial Center 1979). See S. Rep. 96-553, 96th Cong., 2d Sess., pp. 1236-1237 (1980); Kennedy, The Sentencing Reform Act of 1984, 32 Fed. Bar News & J. 62, 65, 66 n.73 (1985).

Page 1126. At the end of Note 4 insert:

The federal Sentencing Reform Act of 1984 abolishes early release on parole but provides that the sentencing judge may, at the time of sentencing, include in the sentence a requirement that the defendant serve a period of supervised release after completing his term of imprisonment. See 18 U.S.C. §3583.